BY BILL BOYLAN:

Network Marketing for Christians

LIFE Giving

Friends Forever

Him 'n me (autobiography)

HEAVEN
OUR HOME
SWEET HOMELAND

Bill Boylan

LifeRich Publishing is a registered trademark of The Reader's Digest Association, Inc.

LifeRich Publishing books may be ordered through booksellers or by contacting:

LifeRich Publishing
1663 Liberty Drive
Bloomington, IN 47403
www.liferichpublishing.com
1 (888) 238-8637

ISBN: 978-1-4897-2442-7 (sc)
ISBN: 978-1-4897-2440-3 (hc)
ISBN: 978-1-4897-2441-0 (e)

Library of Congress Control Number: 2019914281

Print information available on the last page.

LifeRich Publishing rev. date: 10/14/2019

This book is dedicated to my sister, Barbara Lee (Bobbie) (1934–63), and to my newborn daughter, Heather Lee, who lived only a few moments after being born. Both of them now live in the amazing place I visited on March 6, 2018—and are waiting for me to join them there!

Hope is your solid assurance of entering heaven's eternal realms.

—*Colossians 1:5 (Paraphrased)*

CONTENTS

Foreword ix
Preface. xiii

1 How My Visit Happened 1
2 My Visit Begins 5
3 God 9
4 Waters. 19
5 The City. 27
6 Redeemed Humans 41
7 Typical LIFE in Heaven 47
8 Spiritual Activities. 55
9 Dining. 61
10 Former Pets and Other Animals 65
11 Music, Other Arts, and Entertainment 69
12 Climate, Topography, and Energy 81
13 Architecture 91

14 Kingdom Economics. 95

15 Children. 99

16 Education 101

17 The Universe 105

18 Vegetation and Trees 111

19 Spiritual LIFE 117

20 No Sin and No Evil 123

21 Dying and Death 131

22 Final Notes 135

  Epilogue. 153

  About the Author 155

FOREWORD

I FIRST MET BILL OVER THIRTY YEARS AGO WHEN A mutual friend organized a small Bible study group in my home. Bill was the teacher. After studying together for a few months we went our separate ways, and Bill and I fell out of touch until about four years ago.

Bill and I started meeting weekly as friends on a one-on-one basis to discuss our thoughts and discoveries about life in general, and share our ramblings about God and our ongoing relationship with Him.

Through our growing friendship I became aware of the books Bill had written over the past twenty years; when I read them I discovered his writing style is that of a down-to-earth teacher with practical applications, and is somewhat homespun in nature. This style reflects his background and life—his early years were lived mostly on a cattle ranch until his teen years. During the years since, he has been employed as a public school and technical institute teacher, a medical administrator, and served many years in the active and reserve military.

In addition, he has gone on a number of short-term mission trips around the world. He continues to teach Bible study classes and has been involved in various other types of ministries through the years. He also has an online presence that contains numerous teachings about biblical subjects and related concepts.

The book you are about to read is not based on Bill's teachings and Bible background. If you compare the writing style in this book to his previous writings, they do not match up. The descriptive writing in this book is wholly out of character with his practical teaching and writing style. I believe this book is a "revelation" from God to Bill. He simply recorded what he observed and experienced during his visit to the future kingdom of God on the restored earth. God used Bill's past writing experiences to serve as a foundation and to prepare him to accurately report and record his visit to heaven.

—Gunar Dzintars
Professional Engineer
August 2018

THE FIRST AND PRIMARY THING I WANT TO SAY about Bill's "transportation" to the unseen realm of a restored earth is that I believe him. Though we've only met once in person, I feel one with him in spirit. Our relationship spans a decade of email communication and frequent phone conversations.

What stands out is Bill's strong faith and commitment to prayer, along with his very sensitive heart to the Holy Spirit about what he believes God has revealed to him in his prayers for my wife and me through the years.

Bill is a prophetic believer, one who believes in miraculous interaction with the Holy Spirit. There have been times when I was struggling with a decision, and I would ask Bill to pray with me about it. He would lovingly immerse himself in prayer over the matter (and even spend some time fasting) and then not hesitate to give me his impressions. He always does so in a very loving, sensitive, and humble way. Usually, when I prayed more about the matter, after having heard Bill's perceptions, I would realize that he likely did hear God's heart in the matter. So my confidence in Bill has grown over time.

Bill is transparent and lays his life before us in his autobiography. He does not hesitate to reveal his difficulties, challenges, and failures. He seeks to impress no one but lives for God's pleasure. Read his autobiography, *HIM 'n me: The Life Journey of a Very Ordinary Man*, and decide for yourself if this is a man you can trust when he writes of heaven as he does.

Bill explained to me that his heavenly experience pertained to what awaits us *after* God becomes "all in all" (1 Corinthians 15:28). If you want to get an idea of what might happen between life on earth and that final state, Bill and I suggest Michael Phillips's novel *Hell and Beyond*.

May God fill your heart with hope, great peace, and joy as you reflect on Bill's report about his amazing visit to heaven.

—Gerry Beauchemin
Author of *Hope beyond Hell* and *Hope for All*
September 2018

PREFACE

> My hope for the future is in a Person, not in fantasy "end-time" events various people predict will occur.
>
> —*Bill Boylan*

RECENTLY, JESUS INVITED ME TO VISIT HIS FUTURE kingdom of heaven "headquartered" on the freshly restored earth—having a majestic city as its capitol. This is the report of my visit.

Why was I invited to visit heaven? Maybe it was only to report my observations and experiences, to give authentic hope to people about the reality of going to God's heavenly kingdom after their physical death. I hope this report helps people look forward without fear and doubt to going to heaven beyond death's dark, fearful, and unknown passage.

My visit is really too incredible to describe in limited human language; in a way, these inadequate words lessen the wonder of my visit. I simply do not know enough superlative words to fully capture what I experienced. Nevertheless, this report is a product of my obedience to God even though I am not fully able to describe my experiences. This report barely opens the door of heaven for a peek inside, so to speak.

My prayer is that whoever learns about my visit will gain genuine assurance and know that heaven is a real, tangible, palpable, material, and livable place where they will go when they die.

As I began to finish writing this manuscript in its final form, I honestly was not sure what God wanted me to do with it—file it away in my computer for now, share it personally with family and friends, or inquire about having it published as a book.

I had some fears about having it published, thinking some people might feel I was mentally or emotionally ill and had a hallucination. I felt that some people might ridicule me.

Then, inside me, I began to feel God saying something like this:

> Bill, my strong desire is for your visit to heaven to give HOPE to people—genuine hope. Especially to multitudes of people who have lost hope (or had it leached out of them) and those who feel no hope whatsoever.
>
> People need hope, not merely to survive in life but to thrive beyond simply existing day by day; they need a sense of meaning and purpose based on hope. For people to live—really live!—they need hope.

I want people to find peace, joy, and contentment—as well as hope—knowing about their wonderful futures in my kingdom on restored earth after they die. I want people to be able to set aside their anxieties and fears about dying and death, replacing them with my HOPE!

Without hope, many people believe death is the end, and all will be lost—forever! With God's hope in them as an anchor for their lives, people can take a deep breath, relax, live their mortal lives the best way they are able to, and know all that is good in this mortal life will be restored in Jesus's coming kingdom. Death will not be an end but a new beginning!

Without really knowing why, many people have lost hope because of what an Italian poet wrote seven hundred years ago! In the early 1300s Dante Alighieri wrote an allegorical poem about the afterlife and hell titled *The Inferno*, in which he wrote these untrue words: "Abandon hope all ye who enter here."

For seven hundred years, thousands (perhaps millions) of people have wrongly believed that statement about hell to be true. On the contrary, in Jesus's kingdom on the restored earth these words are true: "Take hope all you who enter here." Yes, God offers genuine hope for all!

As memories of my visit to heaven slowly surfaced during the few months after my visit, I filled pages and pages with random notes. I wondered whether I should attempt to format them or place them in categories. At first, it seemed all the memories defied any order—there were just too many of them.

Then I began to see some broad categories slowly emerge; these are most of the chapter headings in this book. I realize some of my memories are still very loosely categorized, and some of them I added in the final chapter.

I did my best to put them together in a meaningful way. Above all—no matter the placement of all my memories—I pray that when you learn about my visit to Jesus's kingdom of heaven on the freshly restored earth, it will help you find hope for a bright future for yourself and all those you love.

1

HOW MY VISIT HAPPENED

> Then I looked, and, oh!—a door opened into Heaven. The trumpet-voice ... called out, "Ascend and enter."
>
> —*Revelation 4:1, The Message*

IT WAS A TYPICAL SPRINGLIKE, LATE WINTER DAY: March 6, 2018, at about two o'clock in the afternoon. I was sitting in one of our living room recliners.

I was staring through our front bay window at a beautiful and tranquil scene. Across the street a small rabbit was nibbling on some fresh green blades of grass in the front lawn of our neighbors' home, as a light blue sedan traveled east on our street.

In our front yard some tiny buds were beginning to form on our young Linden tree, in which sparrows flitted among the branches. Our neighbors' pickup truck was parked at the curb in front of their home.

Two children walking by were laughing and giggling, while hop-skipping on our front sidewalk. Above, white fluffy clouds drifted across the bright blue sky.

My wife, Anne, was away, vacationing on the Gulf Coast with our daughter, Sharon. At the moment, I imagined them strolling barefoot on a sandy beach, enjoying warm, salty breezes wafting in from the Gulf of Mexico.

For a few moments I was sipping a cup of hot tea between some household chores. I wasn't napping, dozing, in a state of reverie, meditating, or thinking about anything in particular—just sitting and staring out the front window.

Suddenly, without any forewarning, I noticed a curious shimmering, fluttering, and waviness in the room directly in front of me. My entire living room seemed to shift from level to a slight angle. I did not feel any fear.

SOMEWHERE ELSE

Instantly, I was elsewhere, standing on the near bank of a wide, crystal-clear river flowing lazily in front of me, so wide I could not see the far bank. I was in another place, another dimension.

Turning, I could see myself still sitting in my recliner, yet some part of me was standing at the river's edge. I was me, but some part of me was no longer in my recliner.

I knew I was not having a near-death experience (NDE). I wasn't hallucinating, having some sort of schizophrenic episode, nor was I in a trance. I was fully alive, conscious, rational, and sane. I did not suddenly become mentally ill. Something within me simply accepted at face value that I had become a visitor to God's kingdom of heaven without having died.

Since I had not died, I did not experience rushing upward through a tunnel of some sort—toward a bright light at the end of the tunnel, as many people who have had NDEs have reported happened to them after they had returned from near death.

Like Paul the apostle wrote, whether I was in my physical body or out of my body, I honestly don't know; all I know is that the person in the recliner and the person on the riverbank were both me, and were asking, "Where am I? What's going on? What's happening to me?" In spite of my questions and mild uneasiness, I was experiencing a sensation of wonderful peace.

2

MY VISIT BEGINS

> There are coming heavens new in quality, and an earth new in quality, where righteousness will be fully at home.
>
> —2 Peter 3:13, TPT

STANDING ON THAT RIVERBANK, I HEARD A CLEAR voice from my immediate left and turned toward its source. Standing there was a being—human-like, but not: about eight feet tall, stately, well-built, semitransparent, and glowing from the inside. The being's outward physical appearance was that of a male, but I honestly could not tell if he was human, an angel, or some other species. Wearing ordinary casual clothing, he stood a few feet from me.

I knew he was not some sort of alien or science fiction creature. He was not a ghost or phantasm; he displayed no hint of evil or malevolence. I knew he was not an android or hologram. This being standing beside me was very real.

We held hands a lot during my visit and spoke often with one another. Most of our communication was in the form of him answering my questions. He was intelligent, loving, gracious, and friendly. Revealing his name, he said: "I am Alaleel."

He did not always answer me because in my heart I knew there were some questions he was not allowed to answer. Those that he did reply to, he did so immediately, usually through some sort of telepathy. It was like he was directly communicating to my spirit. However, when he chose to speak aloud, his voice had healing qualities, with a soothing rhythm and pitch. He said to me: "Bill, God has invited you to visit heaven; I am your escort—your tour guide. Welcome to God's kingdom of heaven on the freshly restored earth!"

GOD'S KINGDOM OF HEAVEN

I somehow knew I would be visiting only a tiny portion of God's kingdom of heaven based here on the restored earth—the entirety of the remainder of heaven being boundless, infinite, beyond measure, and eternal. The small portion of my visit on the freshly restored earth was a microcosm of the limitless kingdom of heaven—the "kingdom come" of which Jesus spoke and for which millions of people have been praying for many centuries.

During my visit I learned that in a broad sense, the entire infinite universe is humanity's future heavenly home in eternal realms, but in a narrower sense the freshly renewed and restored earth is our true native homeland. It seemed to me that the restored earth I was visiting was merely the starting point, the seed plot of God's universal kingdom of heaven spreading infinitely throughout all creation. Restored earth is home base for redeemed, resurrected, and restored humans, but eternal LIFE is everywhere God is: in unlimited, eternal realms. Wherever God is, His kingdom is—and all His beloved, redeemed human children are where He is!

As we stood on the bank of that wide river, my escort told me, "God has invited you to visit heaven so you can report back your experiences and observations while you are here. People within your sphere of earthly influence want to know what their future in God's kingdom of heaven will be like—in practical, realistic, tangible ways— not necessarily the spiritual, ethereal, nontangible aspects of LIFE in heaven."

VISITORS AND CITIZENS

During my visit, other visitors were being escorted around the kingdom of heaven on the freshly restored earth just as I was. Although they were not visible, I simply knew they were there—hundreds, perhaps thousands, from other societies, cultures, and eras, all seeing the same phenomena but each of us from differing perspectives. It's difficult for me to explain: God's kingdom is the same for each visitor, but each visitor sees it through different eyes.

The same is true for the kingdom's redeemed citizens. Each one's experience is based on his or her old earth locale and times in which he or she lived. Yet each citizen is right at home interacting with every other citizen in spite of widely differing backgrounds and experiences on old earth. Their vast differences do not result in any problems interacting and knowing one another. There are no language barriers. In spite of all differences, in the Spirit there is instant oneness, unity, and full acceptance of one another.

CROSSING THE RIVER

My escort asked, "Are you ready?" Before I was able to reply, we had instantly crossed that wide river and were standing on the far side in a land of wondrous beauty that few mortals had ever visited.

It was a bright, clear day, but the brightness did not emanate from the sun. There were slight breezes carrying pleasant, flowery scents I had never smelled before. I could hear soft, pleasant music coming from an unknown source far away, yet it resounded everywhere.

My visit to God's kingdom of heaven on the restored earth had begun!

3

GOD

> All who were standing around the Throne—Angels, Elders, Animals—fell on their faces before the Throne and worshiped God, singing:
>
> "Oh, Yes!
> The blessing and glory and wisdom and thanksgiving,
> The honor and power and strength,
> To our God forever and ever and ever!
> Oh, Yes!"
>
> —*Revelation 7:11–12, The Message*

GOD AS FATHER

THERE COULD BE NO MORE EXCITING WAY TO BEGIN my visit to the kingdom of heaven on the restored earth than to observe and learn more about God than I could ever have known as a mortal on old earth!

In Jesus's kingdom of heaven, redeemed citizens are

always extolling and lauding God with expressions, exclamations, and shouts of praise, joy, prayer, wonder, and awe.

I did not see God, nor did God as Father ever appear to me, but while visiting heaven I was always keenly aware of His pervasive unseen presence of unconditional, relentless, unbounded love beyond measure. God's love is the law of the land.

In His kingdom, God is sovereign in an absolute sense. He is finally and truly known and acclaimed as Creator and Supreme Being over all His creation.

The LIFE of God, sovereign Creator of all, permeates, maintains, and sustains all of creation. In a sense, in His heavenly kingdom, God's LIFE is far more tangible and palpable, more present than we ever experience here during this mortal life.

(Note: Because of the eternal LIFE of God—His very own Self-existent LIFE—which suffuses everything in heaven, I have chosen to capitalize LIFE throughout this report.)

During my visit to heaven, I finally understood that God shall ever be infinite God, Creator of all, but in that wonderful land beyond full human description, redeemed and restored humanity are godlike within their own finite spheres of influence allotted them by God.

Even though I never saw God during my visit to heaven, I know He is pure, unapproachable Light and total Energy. For a human—mortal or immortal—to approach near to God would cause them to be instantly burned up and consumed into nothingness.

The only Person who can stand in God's overwhelming, fiery Presence is Jesus, the exact visible image of God.

Humans are created in God's image as visible representations of the invisible God—marred, incomplete representations here, but completed visible representations in heaven.

In God's overwhelming brightness He cannot be seen by His creation, although He is ever-present throughout. God is pure and complete love, grace, mercy, and truth. He is pure Power, always inexorably and irresistibly drawing all creation to Himself—to His loving heart at the center of all.

Only Jesus can see God and reveal God's all-loving character and nature. Yet, in another sense, God is seen in and through His creation almost as much as He is seen in and through Jesus. And, yes, especially in and through redeemed humans who exhibit His character and nature within and through them. The basic essence of God's character and nature is love.

In heaven, God's love is tangible and palpable, expressed fully to all creation through redeemed and restored humans in whom His love is fully resident and from whom it flows irresistibly and unceasingly. God's love is relentless, ever-flowing, never ceasing, never lessening, and always drawing all things in the universe to Him as a magnet draws iron filings to itself.

As mentioned above, LIFE—God's very own LIFE in eternal realms is so much greater and different from any lesser, mortal, biological life we experience during this temporary mortal phase of our existence on old earth.

In fact, in His kingdom on earth, redeemed humans no longer merely believe in God by means of their God-given faith; instead they KNOW Him deeply and intimately in a way never experienced by anyone other than Jesus here on old earth! Now they live by knowing God, not by merely believing in Him by means of faith.

His LIFE energizes, enervates, and pulsates in and through everything from the tiniest to the greatest objects in creation. From atoms and their smallest components to the largest objects in the universe, all vibrate with God's LIFE and energy.

All creation is divinely interconnected by God's LIFE, infused and suffused with God's loving presence. God is not in everything; rather, everything is in God.

It is written in the Bible about Adam and Eve, "They heard the sound of God strolling in the garden in the evening breeze" (Genesis 3:8, The Message). In heaven, the "sound" of God strolling everywhere throughout those eternal realms is heard as background sound everywhere one goes; His sound is heard perfectly as He walks everywhere. It is not necessarily a sound as if hearing God's footfalls, but a musical sound of His very tangible presence everywhere.

GOD THE SON: JESUS

God the Son, Jesus, is everywhere at once, saturating everything, but completely present with each individual as He sovereignly reigns with love and grace over His vast, unbounded creation. In heaven, there is always an overwhelming feeling of love, joy, peace, and triumph over death and hell because of Jesus's completed, redeeming, substitutionary work on behalf of all humanity.

In those heavenly realms, everyone seems to instantly know everyone else even when they meet for the first time. But the person who is best known (and who knows everyone the best) is Jesus.

And He is always recognized by the highly visible scars of the nails in His wrists and ankles and by the deep spear wound that pierced His side during His crucifixion. Even when He wears long-sleeved shirts and ankle-length trousers (or full robes), somehow those pronounced scars still show through His clothing. They are not understood to be excruciating execution wounds so much as they are understood to be the triumphant means by which He secured salvation and entrance into heaven for all humanity.

Sometimes, Jesus wears regular, casual clothing. At other times He wears a glistening, radiant, prismatic, white, calf-length robe with a belt of golden fabric. Jesus does not wear His hair long as many artists throughout history have depicted Him.

At times He appears as an "ordinary" heavenly person, and at other times He shines brighter than the midday sun; it is not a blinding brightness; it bathes people in God's love and warms, soothes, heals, and conveys deep contentment to those in His immediate presence.

Much of the time I observed Jesus hanging out at parties, celebrations, weddings, cookouts, reunions, and the like—laughing, jesting, singing, quipping, joking, and enjoying the company and fellowship of all His redeemed and restored, human brothers and sisters, as well as His beloved animal friends and companions.

He loves to cook and serve at events where there is food, sometimes miraculously multiplying His special dishes when necessary for quickly gathering crowds; no one needs an invitation when Jesus is the host and chef. All are welcome. No one is ever turned away.

He also enjoys playing all manner of sports at various picnics, outings, and events: running, jumping, chasing, participating in races, and similar events.

He especially cherishes children and pays them patient, close, and loving attention, while laughing and telling them stories that He acts out in a lively manner, answering their questions, and enjoying animated sing-a-longs. Most often, when I saw Him during my visit, He was surrounded by children of all ages, all clamoring for His attention.

He wrestles with them, tickles the smaller ones, and plays all manner of childhood games with them; I saw Him on merry-go-rounds with children and sliding down playground slides with a child on His lap. He seems to greatly enjoy zooming down water slides and snow sledding with children surrounding Him.

All children know they can trust Jesus—that He will never hurt them, never betray them, never turn His back on them or abandon them, never be anything but fully loving and kind. They know He is their best friend.

Jesus doesn't greet others with handshakes, back-slapping, or waves of His hand. Instead, He hugs a lot! And when He hugs people—adults and children alike—they know they've been lovingly hugged by God because His hugs actually transmit LIFE into the people He hugs—and that's everyone.

Each citizen of heaven now knows in detail all those blank spots in his or her own salvation stories on old earth. They finally understand what God was so often doing behind the scenes throughout their former lives, both before and after becoming believers in Jesus.

They now see that God was always "standing somewhere in the shadows" sovereignly and providentially orchestrating all events during their mortal lives—always working out all things for their highest good, always filtering all things through His love for them. Through Jesus's unspeakable agony on the cross, all the past sufferings of all creation have finally been turned into good as God promises in the Bible.

Everyone delights in sharing their own salvation histories with others—and listening to those of others—all such stories giving laud, worship, and praise to Jesus who they now know has always done all things well!

Jesus always leads others by humbly serving them, modeling true servant-leadership in all gatherings, in all work and labor, in all relationships, and in all situations. He humbly receives thanks, worship, and praise for serving all humanity—indeed, all creation!—throughout His eternal realms.

For most humans during their mortal journey here on old earth, there is often some sort of separation between us—the created ones—and our Creator. In the heavenly kingdom, there is never any separation between creation and its Creator. All is one; all is in perfect union. All creation is inseparably linked and divinely interconnected down to the smallest subatomic level, all consisting, cohering, and adhering by the unlimited, binding power of God the Holy Spirit flowing through and from Jesus.

Much of the time, Jesus is seen in close company with John, James, and Peter, but, somehow, no one else ever feels excluded from His closest company; He is the loving, closest, best friend to all. And, yes, I saw His close friend and disciple, Judas Iscariot, there, too!

SUICIDE

Speaking of Judas, no one who committed suicide on old earth is excluded from Jesus's kingdom on the restored earth, but they do undergo some sort of brief newcomers intake processing that I did not understand; however, I sensed the processing was because they did not fully expect to enter Jesus's kingdom after they died at their own hands by choosing to give their lives back to God, and some were very surprised they were there.

People can talk with Jesus freely and at length, telling Him all things, disclosing everything, asking Him anything. He is infinitely patient while listening to others. Somehow, since there is no passage of time in heaven, everything that occurs is absolutely simultaneous; in keeping company with people, Jesus can devote His full attention to one person, while, at the same time, devote His full attention to all.

That pervasive simultaneity is difficult for me to explain; I simply experienced and observed its reality. Jesus is localized and fully present with any group, yet He is always present with every individual. I cannot understand that—it is simply the nature of His pervasive presence throughout heaven as God the Son.

JESUS THE TEACHER

Among everything else Jesus loves to do, He is especially fond of teaching. I often observed small groups of people sitting at His feet; usually, the small groups consist of a dozen or so, yet in some mysterious way everyone is present at all times. As He teaches and shares, He pours His very LIFE into His listeners.

Every word He speaks is pure, piercing to the very inner spirits of His hearers—into their deepest inner beings. His words overflow with grace, oozing compassion and healing to the entire beings of His hearers, washing over them in waves of love.

As He teaches, His face shines with a pure light. His eyes pierce with truth. People come away from His teaching sessions filled to the full with His LIFE and wholeness.

Here on old earth, I often yearn—as you probably do—for God's closer presence in my life; it's a tremendous comfort for me to know I will finally experience His all-loving, full presence in His heavenly kingdom on the renewed and restored earth.

GOD: FATHER, SON, SPIRIT

In Jesus's kingdom, there is finally the pervasive awareness (yet never fully understood because redeemed humans remain finite) that God is the Supreme Triune Being, the Trinity: God the Father, God the Son, and God the Spirit.

Jesus is not the Son of God (in a manner of speaking), considered as somewhat subordinate to God the Father. Rather, He is fully God the Son—Father, Son, and Spirit being completely equal in all aspects and all respects! They enjoy the deepest of loving, intimate relationships with one another.

The only way I can describe the unseen Holy Spirit in the kingdom of heaven's eternal realms is to say He is the breath of God, the wind of God, God in action—as He has always been and ever shall be!

COMPLETE RESTORATION

Here on old earth, we generally tend to feel Jesus's sacrifice was to redeem and restore only sinful humanity to full union with God. In heaven, it is understood His sacrifice redeemed and restored much, much more: the entire "fallen" universe. All—All!—of creation has been restored to wholeness and completeness by Jesus. Here, when we restore something (such as those who restore old automobiles), we attempt to restore it to its original condition. God's restoration is always far, far more and infinitely greater than the original condition.

Somehow, I want to strongly emphasize that in Jesus's kingdom, God is All in all, Everything to everyone, having given His very own Eternal LIFE to the entirety of creation. All is included. Nothing is excluded. There is a Greek word for this phenomena: *apokatastasis*. It means that the entirety of creation is filled to the full with God. There is no longer anything that does not have all of God's full permeating LIFE within. All is fully and completely restored, exceedingly greater and beyond its original, created condition.

4

WATERS

> Then the Angel showed me Water-of-Life River,
> crystal-bright. It flowed from the Throne of God
> and the Lamb, right down the middle of the street.
>
> —*Revelation 22:1–2, The Message*

AQUATIC LIFE AND CREATURES

THE FIRST FEATURE THAT IMMEDIATELY CAPTURED
my attention at the very beginning of my visit is the majestic
river beside which I now stood (and—in addition—other
waters in heaven). The great river (and all other bodies of
water) teems with all manner of aquatic life, all of which
swim, paddle, swarm, leap, and often soar briefly above
the waters just for the sheer joy of being alive: fish, turtles,
sharks, dolphins, whales, eels, manta rays—multitudes
and multitudes of aquatic creatures of every size and
description.

I could hear them singing merrily along with the laughing waters in which they live and play. Large and small schools of fish and other aquatic creatures exuberantly frolic and caper together with perfect choreography.

On oceans and seas, large fish and other aquatic animals (tunas, dolphins, sharks, whales, and the like) offer rides to humans—in chair-like apparatuses strapped to their backs and in small skiffs pulled behind them; they swim slowly or fast depending on the preferences of the passengers. It appears to be a joyful experience to dash through the waves either riding upon or pulled by a large sea creature that skillfully swims and weaves through the waters in numberless patterns.

There is no danger in such activities. The aquatic creatures and humans interact and converse with one another with laughter and joy as they glide through the waters.

All water is alive, not merely in the sense of being full and teeming with all manner of living creatures, but water is in itself real LIFE—and LIFE giving!— LIFE flowing from God into all water. All water is potable, nontoxic, and unpolluted.

SOURCE OF THE GREAT RIVER

The headwaters of the great River of LIFE gush from a vast opening beneath the Throne of God and then flow from there as a river to a massive, never-ceasing waterfall cascading from a huge opening high on one of the outer walls of the city; I'll tell you more about the city and God's throne in the next chapter.

ACTIVITIES ON OCEANS, SEAS, AND LAKES

On oceans, seas, and lakes, I saw great floating cities, some with hundreds of thousands of inhabitants. Huge cruise ships ply the oceans and seas. Also, family-sized boats and ships sail and cruise virtually everywhere, not only as habitations, but also for recreation on the waters. Some of the ships are majestic—restored three-masted sailing vessels and other, older types of sea-going vessels such as steamships. Some of the boats and ships are very ancient vessels, fully restored.

Water sports take place in crystal clear, unpolluted lakes and rivers, and oceans and seas. The water's fish and mammal inhabitants join in the sports and festivities right alongside redeemed humans.

All oceans, seas, and other bodies of water range from colors of deep jade green to rich turquoise, from crystal clear to bright silver, to deepest blue.

I saw people gracefully diving from great heights into various bodies of water. Swimmers swim great distances for sheer joy and just for the sport of it. Although most bodies of water are very calm and placid, there are certain areas set aside for surfing in great swelling waves.

All water sports take place in both summer and winter. In various regions and locales, seasons are meteorologically created just for those sports—all similar to a full range of both summer and winter Olympics here on old earth. Such events are all friendly competition at local, regional, national, and worldwide levels. When these seasons are no longer needed for such sports, they miraculously cease.

There are never any accidental drownings, especially from rip currents. I observed much underwater touring, exploring, and human habitations, including underwater hamlets, towns, villages, and large cities.

NO NEED FOR OXYGEN APPARATUS

Redeemed humans and land animals do not need oxygen apparatus in order to breathe underwater; they can remain underwater for any length of time without needing artificial means to help them breathe. I don't understand how this happens—just that it does. They can dive and swim to any depths without harm or injury.

The seas and oceans are never tempestuous or raging; there are no towering waves—no tsunamis, cyclones, or hurricanes over the waters. All waters are always placid and safe. There are no aquatic predators—all aquatic creatures are friendly, playful, and docile, posing no dangers to swimmers or those engaged in water sports.

All people—even small children—can instinctively swim without fear of water or danger from other species in the water. There are no dark and dank swamps, which here on old earth evoke fears and contain many dangers.

Oceans, seas, and other large bodies of water (such as the Great Lakes in North America and Lake Baikal in Siberia) are reconfigured and are all connected by deep, broad waterways.

SPECIAL BRIDGES

Magnificent, ornately painted and decorated bridges span oceans, seas, and rivers from shore to shore. I saw no visible means of support for such bridges to hold them above the waters; they simply float by miraculous means close above the surface of the waters. Nothing is rusted by water.

All the bridges over oceans and seas are quite wide, bearing all manner of foot and vehicle traffic, but periodically along the bridges, there are surfaces many miles wide; at those junctures are small villages and towns where people live who enjoy lifestyles of living near large bodies of water; in such villages are lovely homes, shops, restaurants, and other types of enterprises and businesses.

There is much pedestrian and hiking traffic along the bridges, various types of conveyances (such as tour buses), and animals being ridden. For those who enjoy hiking long distances for recreation and adventure, periodically spaced along the bridges are vast forested areas for camping and relaxation.

NEW LAND MASSES AND ISLANDS

Large land masses (some almost continent-sized) formerly hidden below the surfaces of oceans and seas have risen above the waters, creating huge new habitable and arable areas of land and vast, towering mountain ranges. Since they are new land areas—wilderness areas, so to speak— many people explore them and visit them for pleasure and recreation.

Many citizens of the restored earth live on small islands dotting the oceans and seas; many islands are movable by some means I didn't understand, so the inhabitants can travel from place to place with their homes intact for sightseeing and for water sports and recreation. Water transportation is efficient, fun, and relaxing. Millions live on houseboats both on open waters and along the shorelines of rivers and lakes.

All beaches are beautiful and pristine, having no flotsam and jetsam or other debris, and are lined with fine homes and shops. Beaches are playgrounds for all, both human and animal. In heaven, instead of spending a pleasant, welcome summer at the beach, millions of people permanently live at beaches worldwide.

WATER SPORTS

In addition to the water sports mentioned previously, Jesus participates in all manner of water sports—in and on the surface of water. He especially enjoys beach volleyball, swimming, and surfing. He especially loves foot-races with others on the surface of the waters!

Often I saw water-races between humans and humans, aquatic life and aquatic life, and humans and aquatic life. There is much good-natured jesting, laughing, and encouragement by both participants and spectators at such events.

In most parks throughout the world are small streams, creeks, and lakes. In them, ducks, geese, and swans paddle about, and turtles, frogs, and other small aquatic creatures swim, play, and converse. Often, they invite humans to join them in the water to play and interact with them. Children especially love to wade in the waters, playing and swimming with the small fish, birds, and animals.

Often in parks and other recreational areas, great geysers of living water burst from the earth, spouting from a few feet to a hundred or more feet high. As the geysers bubble and spurt up and down, both people and animals in the vicinity flock to play in them, being lifted up by the strong force of the gushing waters (and then they float down very safely). There is no danger in playing among the huge geysers.

AQUATIC GARDENS

Vast aquatic flower gardens (some many thousands of square miles in size) dot earth's oceans and seas. They are virtually numberless, mixed with colorful coral and similar living creatures growing in the waters. The gardens are designed and maintained by various aquatic creatures such as large fish, dolphins, turtles, and others.

The gardens are open to tourists who are guided through the gardens by all manner of aquatic creatures. As part of the garden tours, large fish, dolphins, sharks, and whales are fitted on their backs with gondola-like apparatuses ridden by tourists as they weave their way through the gardens during the tours.

The Dead Sea and other similar bodies of water such as the Great Salt Lake in North America are no longer "dead." They are full of aquatic life and are favorite resort destinations for people living in those general areas. The Dead Sea is now connected to the Mediterranean Sea by a wide canal traveled by visitors from all over the world.

The great city about which I shall next tell you has a vast harbor where boats and ships constantly arrive and depart from the Mediterranean Sea through the canal connecting the seas.

5

THE CITY

I saw the Holy City, the New Jerusalem, descending
out of the heavenly realm from the presence of God,
like a pleasing bride that had been prepared for her
husband, adorned for her wedding.

—*Revelation 21:2, TPT*

NOW I'M PARTICULARLY EXCITED TO TELL YOU ABOUT
the majestic city! I know ahead of time it's going to be
extremely difficult for me to describe its numerous features.

Three of my favorite authors are George McDonald
and J. R. Tolkien (nineteenth and twentieth centuries),
and C. S. Lewis (twentieth century). They were excellent
descriptive writers of both fact and fiction. With their new,
near-infinite vocabularies, I wish they were here to help me
describe the city to you.

As a matter of fact, I saw all three of those men during
my visit and had the distinct impression they are still

writing excellent fiction and nonfiction—using heavenly languages with far more descriptive words than they knew while mortals!

DESCRIPTION OF THE GREAT CITY

At the outset of my description of the city, I know it is the city described in various places in the Bible, the city whose builder and maker is God! It is the Holy City—the New Jerusalem descended from heaven to earth (Hebrews 11:10 and Revelation 21:2).

The great city is walled, as cities often were in medieval Europe, for example; at times the walls are transparent and at other times are opaque. Sometimes the walls shimmer and pulsate with multihued, intensely bright, pulsating, fluctuating colors—thousands more colors than I have ever seen here on old earth.

Other than the medieval-like walls, in all other respects the city is ultramodern, much like one sees in futuristic, science-fiction movies and television scenes or in some of the most modern cities here on old earth.

I also knew it was the hub city or capital city, not only of God's heavenly kingdom on the restored earth, but of the entire universe, reaching beyond imagination with no bounds. The city is huge, almost beyond comprehension—like a huge cube (or perhaps a pyramid; I could not tell for certain which of the two; the city seemed to shift between the two shapes from time to time) beyond my entire field of vision.

I wrote that it is a huge cube or pyramid; it is—and it isn't. It seems to be such one moment, and then the next moment it is a well-laid out, somewhat typical, horizontal city. It kept shifting in shape and size as I observed it.

It is hundreds of miles long, deep, wide, and high. It has a skyline, suburbs, and environs like most cities here. The city has amazing, towering skyscrapers and other buildings (including individual homes) that seem almost fluid, somehow flowing into and out of one another instead of being composed of solid, completely separate buildings.

Life IN THE CITY

The city's skyscrapers tower out of sight and are of many futuristic shapes and designs. Some are hundreds of stories high! They contain shops, homes, businesses, play areas, parks, theaters, restaurants, and the like, all at various levels set aside as neighborhood groupings in the towering buildings.

Inside the city live, work, and play millions of heaven's citizens constantly coming and going, ranging from workers in the city to visitors and tourists. There are many visitors from others areas and regions of the universe.

Many such beings are constantly coming and going on ambassadorial and diplomatic types of missions—not political—to share God's love throughout the universe. Within the city, a being simply thought of another place in the city and instantly was there. Since I was only a visitor, I was not privileged to travel anywhere beyond the city and earth. Their comings and goings to visit one another are not intrusive or a surprise if they just show up unannounced.

Part of the city, and yet somehow outside the city, are

typical outskirts, suburbs, environs, small agricultural areas, suburban villages, hamlets, and small towns. They are separate yet fully integrated as part of the city. Somehow those outlying areas are much like pseudopods of an amoeba, connected to the city, yet separate. At times the city expands and contracts as necessary in a manner I cannot understand or explain.

There are no pockets of poverty or rundown areas. No garbage or refuse is piled up or strewn about. There are no abandoned vehicles, no unkempt vacant lots, no rundown, deteriorating vacant buildings—either residential, office, or business.

In spite of its millions of inhabitants and tourists and visitors, traffic, commerce, and business, the city is strangely quiet and peaceful at all times; there are no noises comparable to the noises heard in large cities here on old earth.

There is no machine-powered traffic in the city, but there are various other conveyances powered by an unknown and unseen source. There are some gaily decorated horse-drawn carriages (also drawn by other animals, too), but most traffic is foot traffic, flowing smoothly with no congestion I could see.

Those who walk seem not really to walk but, rather, to glide in some manner of ambulatory locomotion I did not comprehend. Many people ride various species of animals for pleasure for both riders and animals. There are what appear to be elongated, pod-shaped public buses and other types of transport vehicles without visible wheels or means of power.

There are no police, fire, or emergency services because there are no situations requiring such services. And no urgent care clinics or hospital emergency rooms.

Since I was only a visitor, I did not enjoy the unrestricted travel of heaven's citizens. I was a passenger of Alaleel. As implied earlier, I never knew if he was a resurrected, restored human or an angel ... or another species of being. I could travel with the speed of thought only when I was with Alaleel.

Doubtless, you have seen television commercials and other photographic images that at first glance seem solid. But as the cameras zoom in closer and ever closer, you can see then that the images that at first appear solid are actually composed of thousands of tiny pixels, all combining to make the solid-appearing images or photographs.

The unique city is that way. At first it appears that all the buildings, streets, and other infrastructure are solid, but at times when I could see more clearly, it turns out that the city is composed of thousands (even millions) of individual people—solid, yet not.

Moreover, as I indicated earlier, the city often shifts shapes. One moment, it seems far away, solid, and horizontal; the next minute it is very close—a gigantic cube or pyramid—and I could see the individual people making up the seemingly solid city. It is fascinating how it recedes into the distance and then appears very close. It is fluid, constantly changing in shape and form, yet seemingly solid at times.

THE CITY A BRIDE

Most fascinating beyond description is that in the process of shifting shapes, one moment it is a city, and the next moment it is a complete, festive wedding scene, with the bride being the main focal point of the scene. A city. A bride. One and the same. As with the city, both the wedding scene and the bride are composed of millions of individual people.

I knew I was seeing an amazing spectacle beyond my limited words to describe. The wedding, the reception, and the marriage supper of Jesus—the Lamb of God—and His Bride are the grandest celebrations of all time and eternity!

As I attempt to describe it to you, it seems very normal and natural for heaven; for here on old earth with its physical limitations, it's almost a science fiction fantasy of shape-shifters and ever-changing forms.

A GREAT TEMPLE

Near the city center, one of the buildings is a huge, museum-like temple patterned somewhat after the architectural plans outlined in chapters 40–48 of the Old Testament book of Ezekiel.

Services in the temple are purely commemorative, with tour guides explaining all the sacrifices, rituals and activities—all pointing to Jesus's perfect and ultimate sacrifice for all humanity, for all creation. As a temporary visitor, I did not attend such temple services and events but was able to view them from a remote location on a large viewing screen in a nearby community hall.

For that matter, not all houses of worship from old earth are on the freshly restored earth—only a few that are most representative of all of them. Those that have been restored are commemorative museums now to show how and why services, rites, and other activities were conducted in such places of worship (of all former religions).

Alaleel reminded me that for centuries on old earth God continually reminded people that He did not permanently dwell in "houses made with hands," although they continued to build houses of worship ranging from temples, to cathedrals, to mega-churches, to individual homes (Acts 7:48–50, 17:24).

Most former leaders of all religions are now popular historians, lecturers, and authors sharing how their particular religion, sect, or denomination once attempted to worship God on old earth. In Jesus's kingdom they now realize their former religions were not so much false as they were incomplete in relation to the completeness found in Jesus and His church on old earth.

HISTORICAL REMINDERS

Numerous guided tours take place throughout the city. In many community theaters, I observed staged reenactments of Holy Week—the crucifixion of Jesus, His resurrection, and return to heaven. Also, the events of the Day of Pentecost are reenacted.

It's not so much that such events are reenacted, but in a sense the audience is actually taken back to observe the original events on old earth at the time they occurred. It is very difficult to explain such historical-yet-not-historical phenomena.

Other major events of both Jewish and Christian history are portrayed—such as the crossing of the Red Sea, the miraculous feeding of many thousands of people by Jesus, and other significant events throughout church history. For example, all the events of the Protestant Reformation are reenacted and commemorated; one can also see reenactments of first missionary journeys into various locales on old earth.

All old earth's history has been swallowed up and transformed into the eternal *now* where all history's events and experiences are finally fully comprehended and perfectly understood by redeemed humanity.

Throughout the city are living museums much like Colonial Williamsburg on old earth. Dioramas seem to be everywhere, not there one moment and there again the next moment. I observed reenactments of various significant events in old earth's salvation history.

Not only in the great city, but throughout all the fair land I visited, there are multitudes of tourist attractions: for example, full-sized replicas of historical objects such as Noah's ark, with real people and real animals aboard.

There were others: King Solomon's magnificent temple, the fishing boat in which Jesus miraculously crossed the Sea of Galilee, the tomb from which the resurrected Jesus burst forth three days after His burial, John Newton's slave ship (now empty, of course), the printing and distribution of the first King James Bible, how and when the Dead Sea Scrolls were hidden and discovered, and many similar historical artifacts from biblical and church history.

I also saw the Dead Sea scrolls in an interactive Museum of the Bible, preserved much as the Declaration of Independence and Constitution of the United States are preserved here on old earth. There are many other historical and archaeological artifacts—Bibles, books, and the like.

I observed one huge museum (occupying hundreds of acres) similar to the Smithsonian Museum, containing historical documents, artifacts, and exhibits. Throughout heaven, there are many replicas, statues, exhibits, and the like of significant items and events throughout human history.

The homes and offices of some former heads of state (such as from the United States, the United Kingdom, Japan, China, Egypt, Persia, various African kingdoms, and Russia) who served or reigned throughout history are museums in heaven, displaying the major historical events and documents of those nations, especially showing God's absolute sovereignty over all nations throughout old earth's history!

THOROUGHFARES

Most of the kingdom of heaven is replete with walking, hiking, and jogging paths and trails through verdant, lush greenbelt areas. There are a few main thoroughfares, all in some mysterious manner exiting from and leading to the gates of the Holy City, the New Jerusalem.

Those main thoroughfares bear descriptive names such as King's Highway, Royal Road, Calvary Road, Jerusalem Way, Highway of LIFE, Boulevard of the Blessed, Hallelujah Avenue, Avenue of the Nations, Avenue of the Redeemed, Victory Row, Overcomer Way, Road to Emmaus, Wilderness Way, Kingdom Way, Highway of Holiness, Grace Drive, and the like.

TWO THRONES

God's throne and Jesus's throne in the city are separate yet somehow coalesce and meld into a single throne—distinct, yet one. Their thrones are always closely surrounded by bright, shining, scintillating, fiery beings: angels, seraphim, cherubim, redeemed elders, and other such beings— countless numbers of them whirling, leaping, dancing, singing, and spinning in complex choreography.

Even though there are so many beings surrounding the thrones, they never block access to the thrones, so that individuals or groups of people standing or kneeling in front of the thrones are alone with our Father and Jesus in spite of the huge crowds of surrounding beings.

The thrones are ornate and splendid, beyond my ability to describe, both resting on massive golden foundations. The foundation of one throne is inscribed with the word *Justice,* the other with the word *Righteousness.*

Both foundations then rest on a single massive stone that seemed to me so large and solid that it could have been the bedrock foundation of the entire universe; a single word, *Love,* is engraved on it. On the glittering wall behind and above the thrones is inscribed another single word in fiery, golden letters: *Grace.*

PRAYER

Ever since I have been a believer in Jesus, I have prayed to God through Jesus, and have long wondered about the mechanics of answered prayer.

While gazing in wonder at Jesus on His throne, I noticed

He caught my eye and glanced to His right; following His glance, I noticed He was drawing my attention to a huge golden door labeled "Supply Room."

An angelic being opened the door momentarily so I could peer inside. It was a single huge room appearing much like a Sam's Club or Costco store with rows and rows of shelves reaching higher than I could see and into the distance farther than I could see.

It is an infinite storehouse full of unlimited tangible and intangible items; I saw multitudes of angelic beings coming and going from the room. Those leaving the room were carrying answers to prayer.

MAGNIFICENT CEREMONIES

Some of the numerous ceremonies I observed taking place before the thrones were "Reward" and "Award" ceremonies. God and Jesus continually dispense rewards to redeemed people who fulfilled assigned duties on old earth; awards are given to people who went above and beyond their assigned duties.

The rewards and awards are not medals or certificates—nothing of that nature. Instead, in some way I didn't understand, they are about relationships the recipients had established with other people in introducing them to God to begin a lifelong and eternal relationship with Him. Rewards and awards have to do with complex, eternal, divine interrelationships between people and with God and Jesus. The relationships to me seemed very complex, spanning multitudes of people and countless generations.

There is a massive city square in front of the thrones

in New Jerusalem, so vast I could not see from one end to the other with my mortal eyes. Massive parades and similar festive pageants and celebratory events are held in the square.

For example, periodically the elders of all new nations around the world travel to New Jerusalem to bring gifts to Jesus, to pay Him homage and swear their devotion to Him. The elders and their large entourages dress in colorful costumes and wave bright banners and flags while dancing, singing, and praising Jesus with loud merriment.

I also observed great schools and pods of aquatic creatures periodically journeying to New Jerusalem to pay homage to Jesus as their Creator; their events and displays of adoration are staged in New Jerusalem's vast harbor. Huge waterspouts and geysers are part of their displays. They swim and cavort in wildly intricate patterns signaling their homage. Bright lights similar to laser lights shine and shimmer from within the waters.

Drawn there by some internal clock, animals also pour into New Jerusalem to worship, laud, and praise their Creator in great festivals and celebrations staged in the massive city square.

It is beyond description to observe the animals leaping and dancing uninhibited in front of Jesus's throne in almost unbelievable displays of prowess, agility, and strength. Often they parade in huge formations of thousands representing each species. Their loud roars and cries are not cacophonous; rather, they all blend together in perfect harmonious praise to their Creator.

On old earth such displays and parades would take countless hours to pass in review in front of the thrones, but in Jesus's kingdom there is no passage of time no matter how long each parade or celebration might last.

BEULAH LAND

In Isaiah 62:4, the Bible names the freshly renewed and restored earth of the future "Beulah Land" (*Beulah* means "marriage") when Jesus finally marries His "bride," composed of all redeemed humanity.

The city, which is also a bride, is the fulfillment of that ancient Old Testament prediction; and simultaneously it is the fulfillment of the New Testament promise when all humanity becomes the Bride of Jesus (Revelation 21:2, 9; 22:17). The festive "Marriage Supper of the Lamb" is perpetual and is enjoyed by all (Revelation 19:9).

In a sense, underlying all the celebrations and festivities held throughout the kingdom of God's eternal realms is that they are all aspects of a universal wedding celebration when all human hopes for a wonderful, loving, and lasting relationship with one another and with God are finally fulfilled.

All background music I heard throughout heaven originates in a massive orchestra hall in the city, but it is heard everywhere; it is not intrusive or bothersome but, rather, is soothing and relaxing to body, mind, and spirit. Such music is continually played in the hall without ceasing: eternal praise music!

6

REDEEMED HUMANS

> God's ransomed will come back, come back to
> Zion cheering, shouting, Joy eternal wreathing their
> heads, exuberant ecstasies transporting them—and
> not a sign of moans or groans.
>
> —*Isaiah 51:11, The Message*

BEFORE I BEGIN TO DESCRIBE REDEEMED HUMANS in Jesus's kingdom on restored earth, I must tell you something Alaleel told me before I even had a chance to think or ask it. I have long suspected that Adam and Eve fell much further than anyone can even imagine. Alaleel told me my suspicions are true. The way redeemed humans are in Jesus's kingdom is exactly the way Adam and Eve were when they were first created—and before their fall. God has simply restored all humanity to their original condition that God planned from the very beginning.

SPIRIT BEINGS

Redeemed human citizens of Jesus's kingdom on the restored earth are spiritual beings patterned after their former biological selves. They do not have skin covering their bodies. Rather, the covering is a substance composed of light. Sometimes, the light-covering appears almost skin-like but is a subdued glow from deep within. Sometimes the light is bright, shimmering, and shining. At other times, the light is overwhelmingly brighter than usual; the person cannot be looked upon by my mortal eyes.

I did not learn why there are changes or differences in appearances and brightness, but during my visit I felt those changes had to do with changing attitudes and feelings of those individuals.

The immortal, redeemed, restored, transformed inhabitants are still human, but far different, far greater, much enhanced from when they were mortals. They are patterned after what they had been as mortals on earth but now having spiritual bodies instead of physical bodies. They seem to be sexless (I could not be certain, of course, but no one informed me otherwise), but nevertheless each was somehow still distinctly male and female.

There were brief times I could see inside redeemed people in heaven and was in awe that instead of blood flowing through their bodies, a form of liquid light has replaced the blood: God's own LIFE-light within them.

I was reminded of Jesus's bright, shining appearance on the Mount of Transfiguration (Mark 9:2) and in the book of Revelation, the last book of the Bible (Revelation 1:13–14).

CLOTHING

There is no need for clothing, since people are literally clothed in light, but the light shimmers with differing colors and hues, always changing to match the prevailing moods of individuals—somewhat like people here wearing different styles and colors of clothing to match the occasion. Even though there is no need for clothing, almost all citizens of restored earth choose to wear colorful, stylish, fashionable clothing they design and fabricate; often clothing is in the form of costumes to celebrate one's mortal heritage or to dress as in living museums.

NEVER GROW OLD

Each person I visited or observed looked somewhat as they appeared just when they arrived in Jesus's kingdom—young or old—yet at the same time each one appears to be in his or her prime. It was almost as if they are shape-shifters to fit various occasions: young, yet in their prime; older, yet in their prime, too.

Heaven's citizens never actually grow old because there is no passage of time that facilitates the aging process. They exist in perfect health and wholeness: body, soul, and spirit functioning in equally perfect harmony and symmetry, with their spirits being "chief among equals," so to speak.

For those who arrive in heaven as newborns, infants, or children, they very quickly grow into prime adulthood but somehow retain their childlike characteristics. In adulthood, they remain childlike but not childish.

All ethnic, racial, genetic, and other types of distinct

human groupings that existed on old earth are still present and obvious among the redeemed humans of restored earth, but there is absolutely no prejudice or bias of any sort! Each citizen of each grouping equally loves each citizen of every other grouping.

I noted one distinction. Those who were Israelites—genetic descendents of Abraham—on old earth seem to have some sort of prominence in heaven, based on their deliberate, outgoing, selfless, above and beyond service to all others. They are loved by God no more than any others, but He is especially fond of them.

HEAVEN'S CITIZENS

Heaven's redeemed citizens are no longer who they once mistakenly thought and felt they were but who they truly are now as completely redeemed and transformed humans in God's kingdom. Paraphrasing what someone once told me: "They know who they are, and they wear it well!"

Also, when people die on old earth and pass to the restored earth, they are newly born in an explosion of light; they now have within them an inner, expanding universe, ever-growing in eternal realms. They once lived in a husk, a shell of a body; now they are whole and complete; their spirits and souls are ever-enlarging in new spiritual bodies patterned after their former physical bodies.

It took me awhile to realize that no one hides any longer behind any false veneers of social convention. Openness, trust, respect, forthrightness, truth—spoken and acted in love—prevail. There is no duplicity, no lying, no stretching the truth, no hiding the truth, no covering up the truth, and no omission of truth. There is only "truth and nothing but the truth."

In addition to people meeting face to face with one another, at times I observed them visiting, talking, and meeting with other individuals or groups by means of what appeared to be some sort of sophisticated holographic displays. They appeared far more real in person and present than we have ever observed here in this life; people might be far away from one another yet immediately present holographically in a way I could not comprehend.

Everywhere I visited—from large cities to small hamlets—there is always a pervasive atmosphere of joy and jubilation, as though something wonderful is always occurring—and it is!

There have been many artistic depictions of redeemed people in heaven—in all sorts of artistic mediums. I instinctively knew redeemed mortals with wings wearing long white robes weren't sitting on fluffy clouds playing harps or engaging in some sorts of holy or spiritual activities all the time, all the while keeping their haloes properly adjusted. Life in Jesus's kingdom on the restored earth is not an eternal Sunday go-to-meeting day!

7

TYPICAL LIFE IN HEAVEN

They'll build houses and move in. They'll plant fields and eat what they grow. No more building a house that some outsider takes over, no more planting fields that some enemy confiscates, for my people will be as long-lived as trees, my chosen ones will have satisfaction in their work.

—*Isaiah 65:21–22, The Message*

HEAVEN'S ACTIVITIES

BEFORE VISITING JESUS'S KINGDOM OF HEAVEN, I used to wonder what heaven's citizens do there forever ... and forever ... and forever ... and ever. As many mortals here do, I held the naïve view that much of the activity in heaven consists of some sort of eternal church service or other types of boring mandatory religious activities.

Many people here on old earth who hold these naïve views do not want to spend eternity in a heaven of that nature. That type of heaven gives them no hope! That was certainly true of me before my visit to Jesus's kingdom on the freshly restored earth.

Now I know what they do in heaven: they laugh, play, visit, study, learn, labor, work, construct, walk, hike, travel, attend cultural and social and athletic events, read, worship God, play musical instruments, sing, join various clubs and group activities, dine, dance in God's presence, and constantly learn new, interesting skills. They continually design, create, and invent.

People are always active except for times when they choose to relax; they do not need sleep, but I did see people relaxing for brief periods. I did not see any instances of what appeared to be laziness.

Many kingdom citizens delight in restoring and customizing vehicles from old earth. They do not seem to have motors such as we understand them but are powered by some other source. Throughout heaven, there are huge gatherings featuring restored and custom vehicles on display—from the very first vintage automobiles to ones newly created by designers on the restored earth.

Redeemed humans also love to restore old art, buildings, and other such features found in Jesus's kingdom. They are always busy redeeming and restoring whatever they choose to work on.

Ordinary LIFE (really EXTRAordinary LIFE!) in the kingdom of God is not ethereal, vague, nebulous, hyper-spiritual, or indistinct; I saw the nuts and bolts, rubber hits the road, ordinary LIFE situations and experiences that citizens in the kingdom of heaven enjoy when they arrive there after their deaths, having made the final transition from temporary mortality to eternal immortality.

No one in heaven is ordinary in the sense we understand the word here. God places His EXTRAordinary LIFE in ordinary people, transforming them into EXTRAordinary redeemed citizens!

There is no overcrowding on restored earth, but only spacious areas for neighborly living and interactions. As mentioned previously, one merely thinks where one wants to be and is instantly there unless one chooses to walk to various nearby locations. There are no traffic jams, no collisions, no exhaust pollution, and no traffic congestion.

Everywhere, there are localized neighborhood groupings of buildings large and small, consisting of homes, shops, public gathering places, parks, cafes, restaurants, offices, and other places of enterprise and commerce.

Homes have exercise rooms, laundry facilities, libraries, kitchens, offices, dens, dining rooms, special gathering rooms, and viewing rooms. Outside are lush, well-maintained yards and gardens, patios with outdoor cooking facilities, fire pits, swimming pools, picnic areas, and similar amenities.

There are no fences between neighboring homes or between adjoining farms, ranches, and fields serving as barriers; people simply seem to know their own property lines and personal spaces.

In those localized neighborhoods everyone seems to know everyone else intimately, and there is much visiting between homes, in shops, and in parks, with people strolling and sauntering about, just enjoying LIFE in general and each other's company. In the localized neighborhood groupings there are small downtown trade areas with craft and other types of shops, offering handmade items.

I observed neighborhood gathering places for the

exchanges of wares and ideas, Bible studies, lively discussion groups, heartfelt prayer meetings, and the like. I saw people meeting in book clubs, writers groups, and other types of groups for people with shared interests: artist guilds, travel groups, gatherings for public and motivational speaking, for all manner of hobbies, and groups organized to selflessly serve others in various ways.

Here on old earth, I enjoy my community library and appreciate its staff. In Jesus's kingdom, at first I was disappointed that I did not see any libraries. I asked Alaleel why there weren't any. He then showed me small machines (much like our ATMs) in homes, shops, and businesses where people could order limitless e-books and regular books from both old earth and new ones written by authors in heaven.

FAMILIAR SCENES

I often saw people visiting on front porches, with the familiar—to me—creaking of porch swings, the swishing of rocking chairs, and even slamming wooden screen doors in situations familiar to me on old earth.

I observed other similar scenes, too, but they were not necessarily familiar to me because of the geographic, ethnic, or racial backgrounds of those people I saw in such scenes.

In other words, each such homey type of scene is familiar to people with that same background, while not necessarily being meaningful to others without that specific background, history, and locale on old earth.

All that I observed and experienced somehow was

tailored to me—to the times in which I lived on old earth, to where I lived, and among whom I lived, worked, and played.

Similarly, I knew during my visit that other visitors were observing and experiencing the same events and situations as I was, but the same scenes I saw were adapted and tailor-made for them so that what they were seeing and experiencing was altogether different from what I observed and experienced.

I'm having great difficulty explaining that. I was observing and experiencing things and events based on my life on old earth the in twentieth- and twenty-first-century United States. Others were observing and experiencing similar things but based on their lives, say, in fourth-century Asia: similar events, but different perspectives based on our different lives on old earth.

TIMELESS

There are no clocks, watches, timepieces, or other devices to measure time, because there is no passage of time. Heaven is a realm of timelessness, of absolute simultaneousness, not a state of unending time. Appointments are kept by some sort of internal knowing about when and where to be somewhere.

There is no pressure or stress to accomplish tasks on time, to keep tight schedules, or to be somewhere at specified times, but everyone always seems to be where they are supposed to be when they need to be.

MISCELLANEOUS LIVING

I observed many construction projects much like neighborhood barn raisings on old earth, with much laughing, picnicking, singing, and fellowshipping as the structures are being built.

Throughout the kingdom of heaven I noticed there is much use of spectacular fireworks during certain celebrations and events—fireworks that soar higher into the atmosphere, are much more colorful than any on old earth, linger longer in the skies, and spread out across the skies in a much more spectacular manner. No accidental explosions or fires mar such occasions.

I observed numerous pageants, celebrations, and festivals—all with much feasting. There are historical and commemorative celebrations of individual heroism and celebrations of neighborhood, community, and regional accomplishments—all with only friendly competition. Flags, pennants, banners, and posters wave everywhere one looks.

People who suffered divorces on old earth now fully understand the roles and responsibilities each spouse played in causing the divorce. Formerly divorced persons are now content and at peace. They are loving friends.

Reunions seem to occur almost all the time and are held almost everywhere; they are joyous and are held by both small and large groups. I longed for a reunion for me, but of course there could be none for me yet, since I hadn't yet died and arrived in heaven—my true home.

At such reunions, there are never again any sad farewells or goodbyes—no more sad wrenchings apart or partings with loved ones and lifelong friends. During those glad reunions, all lost and broken acquaintances and friendships are renewed and deepened. Mortal lives on old earth seem to be an endless sequence of painful partings; there are no such partings on restored earth.

No one is an illegal alien; everyone is there legally, their rightful citizenship in heaven bought and paid for by the ultimate sacrifice of Jesus on the cross.

There is never a stranger about whom to be suspicious. As people gather there, they know they will never again have to say goodbye. The reunions are always far greater and far beyond any reunions on old earth. They are great festive parties with the newly arrived citizens as feted guests of honor.

I did not observe any toilet facilities for human bodily waste, nor did I ever see any such animal waste anywhere during my visit.

8

SPIRITUAL ACTIVITIES

> You are worthy, our Lord and God, to receive glory, honor, and power, for you created all things, and by your plan they were created and exist.
>
> —*Revelation 4:11, TPT*

IN JESUS'S KINGDOM ON RESTORED EARTH, HE IS everywhere at once, yet localized so that He can be with and give His full attention to any individual. Often, I see Him going on long walks visiting with individuals—on city streets, through city parks, down the streets and lanes of smaller towns and hamlets, through fields and meadows, and on hiking paths and trails in the countryside.

Often those paths take the walkers near streams, creeks, rivers, and other bodies of water dotting the countryside. On more than one occasion while Jesus strolled down a path or lane with someone, if they came to water they simply kept on walking right on top of the water as if the path simply continued on in that direction!

Also, on numerous occasions at parties or similar events, Jesus and His friends use the surfaces of lakes or other bodies of water as dance floors, dancing there just for the sheer delight and joy of doing so. It was very strange for me to see that happen, but I could feel their joy and gladness; all the while I breathlessly waited for them to sink under the water.

WORDS OF LIFE

When words are spoken aloud in heaven, they always convey uplifting LIFE, health and well-being, and carry love, grace, and truth to build up, strengthen, and encourage the hearer. Spoken words are not mere sounds but are palpable and tangible instruments of goodwill, encouragement, and well-being one to another. One's spoken words are always—always!—creative and LIFE giving. There are no rumors, and there is no gossip, backbiting, or lying.

While as mortals living on old earth, some of the most fulfilling, most gratifying, most meaningful times ever experienced are engaging in long personal discussions with loved ones and close friends—no matter the range of topics. In heaven, I observed the same types of discussions and interactions, but they are even deeper, richer, more meaningful, and more gratifying. There are no restrictions, no limitations on topics, and no time constraints. There is much more depth of understanding, with more background and context of all topics discussed. No one is ever bored by what others are saying.

All conversations are essentially God-centric without necessarily being religious, "holy," or "spiritual." Everywhere there is rich reminiscing, as people now know everything behind the scenes; they now know the true inner life of one another. There is no guile or duplicity.

All inhabitants know and understood and can speak all heavenly languages instantly upon their arrival in heaven, but since I was a visitor, I did not have that capacity.

Also, much is both spoken and written in languages formerly used on old earth. At any time, people could choose which languages to use: earthly or heavenly.

It seems that all angels, seraphim, cherubim, and other such heavenly beings are multilingual, speaking many languages as well as that universal heavenly language. All languages are soft, lilting, and musical. I never heard, yelling, shouting, or screaming (except by children at play).

A third primary means of communication is some manner of instant, unspoken telepathy, but people in heaven are not able to read one another's thoughts; God alone has that capacity and ability.

TRUE SERVANTHOOD

Everyone is a positive, effective servant-leader of others, depending on each situation requiring leadership. Of course, Jesus is the model servant-leader always present on every occasion to lovingly, humbly serve others.

I observed at length Adam and Eve during my visit. In some respects, they are very ordinary, yet regal and imposing, larger-than-life redeemed humans from which all humanity originated. They are deeply respected and honored by all creation. Above all else, they are among the very humblest of God's servants, serving others with deep humility and compassion. I sensed they serve others in such a manner because they know how high God lifted them from the great depths to which they had fallen, dragging all creation down with them at the time of their fall.

All humanity has been given servant-dominion (but not domination!) over all seen and unseen creation, ever serving creation in limitless, measureless ways; people never grow weary of such servanthood, and it is never diminished. It is never boring or tedious.

DESIRES FULFILLED

People love to explore, to experience amazing adventures, to read great literature, to help others, and to teach effectively. The positive and good dreams, visions, goals, and desires of mortal youth never again slip through one's fingers as they did on old earth as people aged.

All those deep—often secret—longings and yearnings, hopes, and desires people had in their mortal lives: to be a musician, to study science, to have deeper relationships with others, to be athletic, to write meaningful poetry, to be truly loved for oneself, to be an orator, to tell homespun stories, or to write novels—all such legitimate longings, desires, and yearnings are fulfilled in heaven.

All legitimate desires are fulfilled because as people there come to know God more and more intimately, God's desires for them and their desires blend, meld, and coalesce, causing God's desires and their desires to become one and the same.

HARMONY AND PURPOSE

In Jesus's kingdom on the renewed and restored earth, all service, work, and labor is conducted with great joy and contentment because in eternal union with God, His will becomes a person's will, and the person's will becomes God's will. Heaven exponentially amplifies and maximizes all our skills, gifts, talents, and abilities beyond imagining.

Just as separate instruments in an orchestra blend in perfect harmony, so all events, happenings, and citizens in heaven blend together in perfect harmony in all that they do for commerce, relaxation, pleasure, and meaningful service to God.

During life on old earth there are all too often events involving random chaos and mayhem. In heaven all is purposeful, with God always working out everything for everyone's highest good. All work and labor has meaning and purpose.

There is no boredom and dull routine. LIFE in heaven is adventurous and full of meaning around each twist and turn of LIFE. There are always an infinite variety of exciting surprises.

9

DINING

> Wonderfully blessed are those who are invited to feast at the wedding celebration of the Lamb!
>
> —*Revelation 19:9, TPT*

FOODS

ALL FOODS ARE ABUNDANT, NOURISHING, AND bountiful yet nonfattening. All pleasant-tasting foods on old earth are much more palatable here—all those foods we had always loved and had a taste for. "Luscious" describes most of the food I saw. Everyone has enough, and there are no leftovers, no waste. Everyone enjoys and is skilled at food preparation.

I observed that on many occasions the best of old earth's national and regional recipes and dishes are prepared and served, and all people are eager to taste national foods and other new foods prepared by others. No one ever seems to be distressed by food they don't like or that disagrees with them or causes stomach upset. No one turns up their noses at distasteful food.

Everyone is a gourmet cook; no one ever just "throws something together" to eat at the last minute. Tasteful, exotic spices and flavorings that were never known on old earth are used in preparing meals. All meals are carefully planned, skillfully cooked, and exquisitely presented, with fragrant cooking aromas filling the air.

Many people while mortals knew lifelong hunger and even starvation; uncounted multitudes on old earth have even died from starvation. In heaven, no one ever again knows hunger; on the other hand, there is no gluttony.

There is food and sparkling beverages—and sparkling water from the River of LIFE. Always there is dancing and singing with party favors, speeches, adulation, joy, and happiness unbridled. Tears of joy (never of sorrow!) flow freely and copiously.

BEVERAGES

The primary beverage consumed by both human and animal citizens of Jesus's kingdom on the freshly restored earth is Living Water originating in the great river flowing from the throne of God in the New Jerusalem.

The temperature of the water being drunk is always modified to suit the preference of the person drinking the beverage. Some of the drinking water is flavored with natural flavorings to suit the tastes of the consumers.

THE EUCHARIST

No alcoholic beverages are consumed—with one notable exception: virtually everywhere one goes there are often festive celebrations of Communion, also called the Lord's Supper or the Eucharist, always held as an integral part of joyful meals of thanksgiving. Wine is drunk at these events.

Jesus is the central figure at each Communion-event. He does not reenact His death on the cross, but at each celebration He explains in eternally deeper and deeper ways the true meaning of His death on the cross. Great praise and thanksgiving generally erupt after Jesus's ongoing explanations of the significance of the cross event.

10

FORMER PETS AND OTHER ANIMALS

> The wolf will romp with the lamb, the leopard sleep with the kid. Calf and lion will eat from the same trough, and a little child will tend them. Cow and bear will graze the same pasture, their calves and cubs grow up together, and the lion eat straw like the ox. The nursing child will crawl over rattlesnake dens, the toddler stick his hand down the hole of a serpent.
>
> —*Isaiah 11:6–8, The Message*

ALL REDEEMED HUMANS ARE ABLE TO COMMUNICATE with most flora and with all animals, including aquatic life. I observed particularly joyful events when people communicated with former pets they had loved on old earth! All former pets are restored to their well-loved human companions; they converse freely and openly, with much talk about their former relationships. Their former owners are no longer owners in any sense; instead, they and their former pets are close friends and companions.

Other cities on the restored earth have normal commerce, as does the New Jerusalem. There are vast greenbelts and parks. I observed no zoos. Instead, animals roam freely, both as beloved pets and as friends of both humans and other animals. No reptiles, insects, or animals are poisonous or harmful to redeemed humans.

All animals that previously had paws, hooves, claws, or pads on old earth, now have rudimentary, prehensile hands enabling them to perform basic tasks requiring such adaptation.

I also observed huge formations and phalanxes of birds flying, swooping, and diving above Jesus's throne with unbridled joy and delight—singing, warbling, screeching, cawing, and chirping their homage to Jesus.

SNAKES

Speaking of animals, I observed snakes (for which I have a strong aversion and unreasoning fear). They no longer crawl and slither along the ground. Rather, their shapes are similar to elongated lizards now, having four limbs (or more, depending on their size and length).

Some walk upright on their two hind limbs, some walk on four legs as most animals do—but some also walk on more legs, again depending on their size and length.

Children especially love to play with the colorful

snakes, often riding the larger ones. Snakes are no longer poisonous or dangerous. It seemed to me that they are even especially grateful they no longer have to crawl and slither as they did on old earth.

11

MUSIC, OTHER ARTS, AND ENTERTAINMENT

Art, music, literature, crafts, technology, clothing, jewelry, education, food preparation—all are part of society or culture, which is the creative accomplishment of God's image-bearers.

—Randy Alcorn, Heaven, 375

MUSIC EVERYWHERE

EVERYWHERE OUTSIDE THE CITIES WHERE THERE ARE more trees, shrubs, bushes, and greenery than in populated areas, I heard bells ringing—soft, lovely, peaceful, tinkling sounds much like those of wind chimes, but I saw no bells or chimes producing the sounds. Yet there is bell-like music—harmonious and melodic, as if played by great handbell choirs. Then I understood: the melodies resound from trees, bushes, and shrubs rustling in the soft, gentle breezes, joyfully praising their Creator!

Everywhere one goes there are little groups of people engaging in spontaneous, joyous festivals of praise and worship, often involving fervent and spirited individual and group interpretive dancing. As mentioned elsewhere, sometimes such dancing takes place on the surfaces of ponds and lakes for entertaining large audiences watching from the shores and from boats.

At various times I heard old-time gospel songs and hymns, southern gospel music, contemporary music both religious and secular, historical Israeli and Christian music, classical music, various national anthems and historical music, and songs sung specifically by angels, seraphim, and cherubim.

There are huge worldwide music festivals where throngs of people gather to play, sing, and listen to their favorite genres of music.

My favorite music here on old earth is southern gospel music, love songs, and ballads from the nineteenth century, Irish music, and Scottish bagpipe music. I look forward to being able to sing and play many types of music, but especially those types, including bagpipes.

ALL CAN SING AND PLAY

I was aware that people such as me who cannot sing well or play musical instruments on old earth are able, in Jesus's kingdom, to sing and play beautiful music. All music is full, rich, meaningful, melodious, and harmonious, sung and played in thousands of languages and dialects. All music, regardless of the style or type, is performed in worship and praise to God; there is no "good" or "bad" music, no sacred and secular music.

Throughout God's kingdom on earth, there are "welcome home bands" and orchestras such as we have here on old earth for returning military service members and heroes. Everyone who dies here and then arrives in Jesus's kingdom is first greeted by Jesus and then by loved ones while majestic homecoming orchestras and choirs resound in the background.

MUSIC AND DISPLAYS BY ANIMALS

The myriad songs sung by birds are lively, cheerful, harmonious, pleasant, beautiful, and lilting—and understandable both to other birds and to humans. The birds sing greetings to one another and praise to their Creator. Interestingly, birds seem to chatter and pass along news about what they see, hear, and do in their daily travels and searches for food—not gossip, but good news about good things they see happening during their daily flights.

They often put on majestic aerial displays, hundreds and thousands of them swooping and dipping through the air in perfect choreography. Sometimes they put on such displays directly above cities, towns, and villages for entertainment purposes during festivals and celebrations.

All birds—from large, majestic eagles to the smallest hummingbirds—get along well with no midair fighting or robbing of eggs or baby birds from one another's nests.

As a matter of interest, all birds that were formerly earth-bound (chickens, turkeys, penguins, etc.) now can fly, and take great delight in flying, soaring, and swooping. Chickens even love to play practical jokes by laying eggs where humans least expect them to be.

All music from redeemed humans, birds, animals—for that matter, all flora and fauna—are blended, harmonious parts of great swelling orchestras and choruses wafting throughout all heaven.

MUSIC HEALS

All heavenly music has wellness and restorative properties—just as a proper massage here has healing properties, and certain music here can soothe and calm at times. Music seems to resonate and reverberate within peoples' bodies and stimulate the tissues and organs of the body in a healthful manner.

In heaven, music is spiritual (God-centered), while here it is mostly soulical (mental) and emotional. Here, our souls and emotions prevail over our spirits; there, the spirit prevails and has mastery—"chief among equals," so to speak.

GOD SINGS

Periodically, God sings special songs to each person in heaven (Zechariah 3:17) in the genre of music that person enjoys most (western, classical, opera, big band, national types, etc). God the Son—Jesus—simply drops by from time to time and sings to that person—always a positive, uplifting song of joy, peace, comfort, encouragement, love, victory, and triumph.

Jesus's song is always a new special song, personalized to fit whatever good things are happening in that person's life just then. It is the Song of songs—the Song that breathes LIFE into all creation. In fact, Jesus's Song of songs carries its recipient back before creation and beyond time into new beginnings in eternal realms.

When God sings to people, His song resonates and reverberates within them, harmonizing and vibrating at the very core of their beings, readjusting the atomic structure of each cell, imparting well-being, strength, LIFE, and wholeness each time He sings.

VARIOUS HEAVENLY MUSIC

I saw minstrels, troubadours, and small vocal and instrumental groups, the purposes of which are to travel throughout the restored earth singing, playing, and performing for others. In villages, hamlets, towns, and cities, neighbors gather spontaneously for neighborhood music jams and sing-alongs.

Many of heaven's inhabitants are innovative composers and music leaders. I saw and heard played musical instruments I had never seen or heard before. I heard and viewed great operas extolling all the works and ways of God. Everywhere are concerts celebrating great events in salvation history.

I listened to innumerable songs written, played, and sung about what Jesus has accomplished for all humanity. Creative, innovative musicals are performed. Angels, cherubim, and seraphim (and other heavenly beings) are often seen and heard blending their instruments and voices with human musical endeavors in great pageants of praise and extravagant worship melodies and songs. All music is rich, full, and satisfying to the redeemed human spirits, minds, and feelings.

Songs that had once been treasured national anthems are now sung along with local and regional songs celebrating the best of rich musical heritages and fond memories of all that had previously been good while people were still mortals.

In concluding my memories about music I heard in heaven, there is always glorious, joyful music in the air, and the atmosphere is ever filled with happy songs. One cannot go anywhere in the vast universe where there is no music. It is never too loud, intrusive, disruptive, or disconsonant, but always heard in the background, always in praise to God, uplifting, and positive.

MUSICAL DESIRES FULFILLED

When on old earth as mortals, people had yearned and desired to possess and display certain skills, talents, gifts, and abilities (such as musical, for example); all such legitimate desires and dreams are fully realized in heaven.

For example, someone who could not sing well on old earth, in heaven can sing and perform beautifully—singing for sheer pleasure, performing for friends and neighbors, and even presenting public concerts. Many people play musical instruments they had always yearned to play while on old earth.

For example, here I have always enjoyed listening to recorded music from the United States's nineteenth century. On restored earth, I fully expect to play and sing such music to my heart's content. I also look forward to singing and playing Irish and Scottish music I have long loved and enjoyed!

GOD'S UNIVERSAL DISPLAYS

This is virtually indescribable, but I observed it on several occasions: God, angels, and other heavenly beings often put on vast displays throughout the universe, temporarily rearranging stars and galactic patterns in dazzling displays (similar to fireworks) as entertainment for citizens of the restored earth—usually to mark or signal some famed event in history or some type of breakthrough or momentous event elsewhere in the universe.

During such massive displays, music resounds throughout the restored earth and the universe—music unlike anything any mortal has ever heard: a blending of whirling, spinning galaxies, singing stars, angelic voices and instruments, and the musical sounds of other heavenly beings, both visible and invisible.

OTHER ARTS

In other areas of the arts besides music, I observed beautiful pottery with multitudes of patterns unlike anything seen here on old earth. Often, people were seen bending over their potter's wheels and working at their kilns as they produced unique, creative pottery never before seen.

In other areas of the arts, statues of great historical and spiritual personages through the ages of time abounded in homes, office buildings, museums, parks, and historical malls. All statues usually have someone nearby who explains to visitors the significance of the statues much as museum or art gallery tour guides do.

Most everyone possesses gifts and talents to paint, to draw, to sketch, to sculpt, and to create other various forms of art using an almost infinite variety of artistic mediums. In some manner I could not understand, much art of that nature is holographic and very lifelike. Most art I observed is what is termed "realism" here.

FRACTALS

Since I first heard of and viewed some painted fractals a few years ago, I've been fascinated by their stunning beauty, complexity, and clarity; I have felt they're almost otherworldly. Now I know they really are otherworldly—heavenly.

I do not understand them, only that they are complex geometrical computations, calculations, and formulas generally depicted as incredibly complex designs. Only a handful of mathematicians and physicists here on old earth understand them even to a small extent.

In God's kingdom, I observed fractals in many locations: some as forms of artistic graffiti, some as wall hangings in home, shops, and museums, and some in art galleries. I often observed them at auctions, trade fairs, and upscale retail shops. Those created by children (!) are most stunning in their beauty and complexity—and simplicity.

I only mention them in this report because during my visit to heaven, I was led to understand that in a manner of speaking, mathematical fractals are God's basic building blocks of both the microcreation and macrocreation. In His infinite imagination God inspires His redeemed children to create fractals and then speaks or sings them into existence as objects or living beings ranging from vast, almost measureless galaxies to the smallest components of atoms.

ANIMAL ARTS

Now that many animals (land, aquatic, and air) have a form of prehensile hands, some of them are also amazingly gifted in all sorts of artistic mediums. Elephants and bears especially excel in painting, using wonderful colors and mediums—especially large murals. Birds often paint birds-eye scenes seen from above—very detailed and colorful landscapes. Dinosaurs paint and sculpt scenes and events from their lives on prehistoric old earth.

Former pets seem to delight in painting humorous and comical scenes from when they used to play tricks on their owners; they even stage theatrical productions of such events.

Those of the simian species excel in creating and designing highly complex paintings (including fractals) and in teaching humans and other animals about their form of art. God often seems to then breathe LIFE into their fractals, creating ever new expressions of art.

Even insects such as ants and termites bore numberless artistic patterns and mazes below ground in the earth, even staging demonstrations of their methodical teamwork and work ethics—as do bees, wasps, and similar insects. There is a unique divine relationship between ants, termites, and other borers—and the earth they love.

ENTERTAINMENT

Television and movies are uplifting, positive, and encouraging, similar to those seen on the Hallmark and nature channels here on old earth; they consist largely of documentaries, biographies, musicals, nature shows, testimonials, and good news about events occurring elsewhere in other cities and locales, including throughout the universe.

All national, worldwide, galactic, and universal newscasts by radio and on television are good news, because throughout heaven only good things happen to good people for good reasons.

There are no video games touting warfare, killing, demons, evil, vampires, zombies, and the like. Rather, video-like games are for friendly competition and mental and spiritual enlightenment and challenges.

ADVERTISEMENTS AND COMMUNICATION

All signs, placards, posters, movies, television commercials, music, menus, and the like are spoken and written in what I perceived to be that universal heavenly language previously mentioned (perhaps many more than one language, actually), which I could neither read nor speak, but I could understand clearly.

I observed no telephones, cell phones, smart phones, or similar types of communication devices. A type of "organic computer" is used mostly for study and research but not for entertainment purposes.

12

CLIMATE, TOPOGRAPHY, AND ENERGY

Let all the universe praise him! The high heavens and everyone on earth, praise him! Let the oceans deep, with everything in them, keep it up!

—*Psalm 69:34, TPT*

RESTORED EARTH INCREASED IN SIZE

BY SOME MIRACULOUS MEANS I DID NOT OBSERVE (but was allowed to know about), God increased the size of the earth by one-fourth its diameter (as one blows up a balloon, increasing its spherical size equally all around).

I knew the enlargement increased the surface of the earth a great deal, but I didn't know how much. After returning from my visit to heaven, I posed a question to two of my friends who are mathematicians, asking them how much the surface of the earth would increase if it were enlarged as noted above.

My friends did some calculations and—without going into great mathematical detail, most of which I wouldn't have understood—informed me such an increase in size would more than double the earth's surface!

Even though the earth's surface more than doubled in size, it was not flattened, enlarged, or distorted, nor did earth's oceans and seas change in depth. I suppose that when such wonderful miracles occur, by their very nature they defy rational or logical explanation.

The enlargement of the restored earth does not affect its orbit around the sun, nor the distances between it and other planets in the solar system. Nor does the enlargement of the restored earth affect the pull of gravity between it, the moon, and other planets in the solar system; tides are not affected either.

In Jesus's kingdom of heaven on the restored earth, fine-china blue skies are always filled with white, cotton-candy wisps of clouds lazily drifting through the bright skies. The atmosphere is always clear as crystal, with no haze, no exhaust fumes, no belching smokestacks, no air pollution, no release of dangerous chemicals, and no smoke from burning forest fires.

Without atmospheric pollution, people can see more stars than they ever saw in their mortal state. There are innumerable billions and billions of stars twinkling on a velvety black background; they spangle the skies with their radiant, multicolored splendor.

TEMPERATURES AND SEASONS

Worldwide, temperatures remain quite constant day and night—very comfortable and temperate. However, when people want to engage in seasonal sports, somehow those seasons miraculously appear in various locales for whatever length of time people want to spend participating in such seasonal sports and activities.

The four seasons continue on restored earth but are milder—less extreme. If people want to build snowmen or throw snowballs, snow miraculously falls. If they want to rake fallen leaves and jump and play in the piles of leaves, fallen leaves mysteriously appear. If they want to bask in the sun and sip iced tea during warm summer days, long, lazy summer days miraculously appear.

People can special order episodes of seasonal weather they prefer for temporary enjoyment. For example, one might order mild, springlike weather with all the pungent smells of newly plowed earth, and trees and flowers beginning to bud. Or, one can order warm summer weather for picnics and special outdoor events. Some enjoy crisp fall weather with the sounds of children playing in specially created piles of fallen leaves. And some enjoy nippy winter weather for winter sports, snowball fights, building snowmen, and creating ice sculptures. All such weather limited to specific occasions can be special ordered for pleasure, outdoor recreation, and other seasonal activities.

WEATHER AND CLIMATE

Fragrant breezes whisper, wafting soft praises to their Creator. Gentle winds sing with glee at their freedom while rustling vegetation laughs with joy along with the passing winds.

Breathing in heaven is different than it is in our mortal state. Heaven's air is greatly concentrated and pure (but never thickly oppressive or muggy), filled with wonderful healthful properties, never polluted, never foul-smelling, never rarified, always the proper mix of gaseous ingredients promoting robust health and unified wholeness—body, soul, and spirit.

There are no destructive weather patterns or environmental disasters: destructive solar flares, massive arable-land-destroying dust storms, flooding, blizzards, freezing temperatures, hailstorms, earthquakes, volcanic eruptions, or droughts that formerly claimed the lives of millions on old earth.

There are no frightening storms with ominous, roiling storm clouds and thunderclouds building beyond the horizon. No deadly flashes of lightning streak to earth. I did not hear any "civil service" alert sirens warning people of impending deadly storms. No children or animals are ever again frightened or terrified by lightning and thunder during dark, scary nights.

However, great roiling, towering thunderclouds with accompanying lightning sometimes form above mountain ranges, but they are nonthreatening, seemingly dancing and flowing together in majestic displays reaching high into the atmosphere.

There are no chaotic weather and climate changes that

plagued humanity on old earth. Climates are predictable, calm, and serene. This feature enhances ordinary LIFE for agriculture, for building and construction, for sports of all types, for travel, and for all enterprise and commerce.

There are no harmful, intense, radiation-laced solar flares spewing from the sun; God adjusted its elements and activities so that the sun is a benign source of heat and light eclipsed by God's Light out-raying from His very being.

There are no stifling hot and dry deserts, yet if people choose to participate in various types of desert sports such as racing with dune buggies or camel racing, deserts miraculously become temporarily available. Areas that had formerly been dry, barren deserts now blossom with all manner of flora in rich, fertile, well-watered, arable soil. The deserts truly do "blossom as a rose," as predicted in Isaiah 35:1.

There is no barren land anywhere. There is no contamination of restored earth: no bacteria, viruses, diseases, pandemics, plagues, pollution from human and natural sources deep within, or unpredictable and turbulent atmosphere that transports spores, dust, pollen, smog, "dirty" moisture and other contaminants.

Heaven's inhabitants do not suffer from weakened immune systems from chemicals, toxins, and pollutants.

RESTORED EARTH'S TOPOGRAPHY

Huge mountain ranges such as the Andes, Rockies, Himalayas, and Alps remain as lofty and majestic as they were on old earth, but in some mysterious manner they are now fully accessible without any dangers for sporting and camping adventures, for tourism, and for habitation for those who choose to live among mountains. There are safe, lengthy cable cars and trams leading to high resorts and mountaintop restaurants and shops.

Mountain climbing is exciting, fun, and adventurous—but holds no dangers for the climbers, some of whom display amazing feats of daring as they climb.

Mountain goats and sheep and other similar animals roam freely among the mountains, interacting and visiting with human inhabitants and tourists. The animals leap and skip among the lofty mountains just for the sheer joy of living and to show off their skills for human onlookers.

AERIAL LIFE

In heaven, there are no motorized aircraft (including helicopters or drones), but are many colorful gliders, soaring hundreds—even thousands—of miles on miraculously directed air and wind currents requested ahead of time by the pilots; the gliders are often accompanied by flocks of birds whirling playfully around them.

And in the skies all over the world drift massive hot-air balloons and dirigibles carrying enthusiasts and tourists in large passenger baskets underneath them, the people observing from the air the many wonders of the kingdom of God on the freshly restored earth below them.

I also observed multitudes of people—young and old—hang gliding and para-sailing, as well as flying with other similar conveyances; entire groups took vacations using such flying devices to travel the world.

Some people have long believed that certain references

in the Bible to earth's future topographical changes are literal; for example "every valley shall be lifted up and every mountain brought low" (Isaiah 40:4). Apparently that is not the case on the restored earth. Most (not all) topography remains as it was on old earth, but in some miraculous way all land is more arable, less rocky, more level, and more productive.

A friend of mine (who is now in heaven) once quipped, "God isn't going to reconfigure the new earth's surface into that of a billiard ball!"

All arable land is more fertile and is watered from underground at just the right moment and in the exact amounts necessary for perfect growing conditions.

UNDERGROUND CAVERNS

Vast, interlinked underground caverns are found throughout the restored earth; they display magnificent features much like those shown to tourists on old earth in massive caverns such as Mammoth Cave in Kentucky and Carlsbad Caverns in New Mexico. Some of the caverns have huge, cathedral-like rooms in which one cannot even see the ceilings above them. And many of the caverns are hundreds—even thousands—of miles in length, some even reaching underneath continents and large bodies of water.

Some people are professional cave explorers and spelunkers for pleasure and recreation, constantly opening up more and more huge underground rooms containing never before seen features with colors in vivid profusion. There are no dangers—including cave-ins or getting lost underground—for spelunkers and visitors.

Unnumbered millions of bats inhabit the caverns and often guide spelunkers and tourists through their vast underground homes, chittering and chattering as they explain various features to their welcomed guests.

FORMER ANTARCTICA

What was once the frozen continent of Antarctica is now a huge, lush, paradise-like, arable land area housing millions of kingdom citizens and vast farms, orchards, vineyards, and gigantic parks for tourism.

Large penguin populations interact playfully with humans. They love to make people laugh at their antics. As noted previously, penguins can now fly, and love swooping and diving in and out of the water from great heights.

Tourists visit huge petrified forests of long-ago ages in former Antarctica. Among some of those forests (both living and petrified) live and play various dinosaurs and other once-extinct animals such as wooly mammoths, for example. Most such once-extinct land animals and air and sea creatures choose to remain in Antarctica as their original home.

It's not necessarily that they are confined there; it's that they are perfectly content to remain there in familiar surroundings. Sometimes they choose to visit elsewhere on restored earth—usually during festive commemorative occasions, with them as featured speakers and often in parades, including aerial displays.

Many people here do not realize that not all dinosaurs on old earth were gargantuan creatures. Some were also small, about the size of some of our typical household pets—some even smaller. On the restored earth, some of those smaller dinosaurs choose to become beloved companions of humans and other restored animals who do not live on restored Antarctica.

Other formerly extinct plants and animals have been restored to LIFE. As mentioned above, many of the larger ones are at home on the vast, restored continent of Antarctica along with many species of dinosaurs. None are poisonous, toxic, or dangerous.

Many of the restored dinosaurs and large flying creatures (such as pterodactyls) give rides to tourists visiting Antarctica, all the while visiting and conversing with their riders, pointing out sights below. Children especially love such rides!

As noted previously, I did not observe any dangerous swamps or areas of quicksand in any parts of the world, and there are no large, unexpected openings of the earth (sinkholes) to swallow objects such as houses and vehicles.

ENERGY SOURCES

In Jesus's kingdom, there is far more than sufficient energy for all of restored earth's needs: from the tamed sun, from safe atomic fusion, and from the natural resources of asteroid mining throughout the solar system; asteroids hold far more raw materials and resources than the entire planet earth holds. Precious metals are used in research and production (not as wealth); organic chemicals and LIFE-giving water are found in abundance on the restored earth and throughout the universe.

Geothermal energy sources power homes and entire

cities from deep underground boiling water and steam. Such natural energy powers various machinery and equipment needed in commerce, research, and development.

In Jesus's kingdom on the restored earth, this seemingly insignificant and obscure planet is finally restored and blessed by God beyond comprehension and is now known by all creation as God's special eternal home.

13

ARCHITECTURE

> Our love for home, our yearning for it, is a glimmer
> of our longing for our true home.
>
> —*Randy Alcorn, Heaven, 334*

HOMES

I VISITED NUMEROUS HOMES; NONE WERE MANSIONS,
only medium-sized to midsized dwellings of various sizes
suited to the number of inhabitants and having no wasted
spaces or unused rooms. There are many styles of homes
representing many periods, locales, and regions in the
history of old earth. All homes are comfortable dwellings
of many shapes, sizes, and colors. It wasn't until I visited
the last one that I realized I hadn't seen any bedrooms in
homes.

There is no false pride in one's home being bigger or
better than the home of one's neighbor. There is no false

pride about living in upscale locales. As was all-too-often the case on old earth, no one is embarrassed by living on "the other side of the tracks." No one strives to live better than others or "to keep up with the Joneses."

Most homes have at least one large room where neighbors gather for social events, Bible studies, book clubs, meetings, for meals, and simply for fun and fellowship. They also have large dining areas both inside and outside with huge tables that serve many.

Some homes have large—almost institutional—kitchens, for those who specifically practice hospitality with food. There are other rooms used for various purposes such as for hobbies, crafts, sewing, art and music, and as workshops for various crafts. Home interiors are tastefully decorated by those living in them.

There is no typical home or property ownership, but some sort of possession I could not understand—all belonged to God but were permanently loaned in some way to their inhabitants. All homes display myriads of bright colors, tasteful art, and gracious, comfortable home furnishings suiting the varying tastes of their inhabitants.

Lights turn on and off automatically as people enter and exit each area of buildings. Although it is always light outside, it seems sometimes that outside light dims to suggest dawn and evening (but never night with total darkness).

Yet even in bright daylight somehow the moon, planets, galaxies, and stars are seen as though it were total darkness. During such dawn and twilight times, ornamental street lights and yard lights turn on and off automatically, turning down to a dim nighttime setting.

HOME FURNISHINGS

Much glass in buildings is similar to what was previously called "tinted glass"—all for privacy purposes. Glass is unbreakable. People can see out, but no one can see in. Some windows seem to be magnifying glasses so people looking out from homes or other buildings can clearly see sights far away.

Personally designed home furnishings and clothing are often produced or manufactured by some sort of devices I can only describe as advanced 3-D printing processes. Homes have individual 3-D printers, but there are also neighborhood shops and even factories with huge such printers to produce larger items.

Photos, prints, paintings, and the like displayed hanging on both the exteriors and interiors of all buildings are in bold, brilliant colors, often are three dimensional, and are "live" in some manner. Some of heaven's citizens have gifts of decorating and are often called upon by others to decorate both the exteriors and interiors of homes, offices, and shops.

GOD IS THE LIGHT

It's difficult to explain, but primary light doesn't come from the sun or from electricity; somehow, all light seems to originate and emanate from God in some manner I could not fathom. There are no hydroelectric dams, no massive and lengthy electric power lines, no unsightly electrical lines (or other types of lines) going into homes and other buildings.

God's light is somehow just there, just present, without any visible means of overland transport from source to user. Coal and nuclear power and natural gas are not used to generate electricity.

Real-time scenes of distant places of interest are displayed on and in homes. Many homes display seasonal and religious exhibits outside their homes, as we display, for example, Christmas and other holiday scenes here on old earth. None of them are garish or in poor taste.

Everything constructed in heaven is permanent and eternal, not subject to decay, decomposition, abandonment, or destruction. Everything has eternal purposes. All is ever new, yet ancient and eternally timeless.

14

KINGDOM ECONOMICS

> Don't hoard treasure down here where it gets eaten by moths and corroded by rust—or worse!—stolen by burglars. Stockpile treasure in heaven, where it's safe from moth and rust and burglars. It's obvious, isn't it? The place where your treasure is, is the place you will most want to be, and end up being.
>
> —*Matthew 6:19–21, The Message*

IN MY LIFE HERE ON OLD EARTH, I UNDERSTAND very little of business, national or international economics, trade, and the like. But in the kingdom of heaven I clearly understood there is no debt of any kind and no need to have any sorts of budgets at any level from personal to international. There are no debt ceilings, no borrowing, and no lending.

GIVING AND RECEIVING

God is the source of all supply, the One who meets all needs, financial and otherwise. People selflessly give to one another as God's instruments or means of supply.

While here as a human, Jesus said, "It is more blessed to give than to receive" (Acts 20:35). Here, many of us practice giving only imperfectly, infrequently, and incompletely. In the kingdom of heaven, giving to others (and serving others) is a basic way of LIFE, practiced perfectly by everyone in every situation—modeled by God, who lovingly gives His all to all.

Giving to one another is the norm, based upon God's giving to miraculously meet the needs of all people through one another. In some miraculous manner, God furnishes the needs of everything and everyone through all people freely and lavishly giving to one another. There are no urgent needs of any kind. At long last, heaven's citizens know the differences between needs and wants.

NO FINANCIAL INSTITUTIONS

There are no electronic devices, handheld or otherwise, to manage money. I saw no use of credit or debit cards, checks, or money orders.

There are no banks or similar types of institutions in heaven, since there is no need for people to save or borrow money, no need for loans, and no need for safe deposit boxes to hide and store money and valuables.

Some people save currency and coins from old earth as a hobby. Also, there is a type of "saving" by people in order to pay extra for various giving projects such as financing field trips for children. No one saves for the future or for a rainy day. No one hoards money. No one is poor or lives in poverty.

There are no national reserve banks for control and storage of national wealth. I saw no massive presses to print paper money or machines to mint coins. For that matter, there is no forestry industry in order to produce all manner of paper products including currency. There are no vagaries of economic depression, recession, or inflation needing controlling by national or international banking systems.

FINANCIAL TRANSACTIONS

There is some sort of giving, sharing, and bartering without overstepping personal boundaries or preferences. There is a form of joyful giving to projects near and far and elsewhere in the universe, but such projects were beyond my understanding as a visitor.

I sensed a pervasive awareness that people enjoy giving far more than they do receiving. No one greedily accumulates wealth, treasures, or goods. People do not need to save for their futures, since in the eternal realms there is no passage of time: no past, present, or future.

There are not any overdue payments, foreclosures, usury, repossessions for late payments or lack of payments, and no evictions. No one has to take out any so-called "payday loans," mortgage their property, or frequent pawn shops in order to get by financially.

There is a widely used form of trade or barter. There

are never any bankruptcies. Everyone has their every need met by God through the giving of others.

In terms of retail sales, there is always truth in advertising, all goods and products are of perfect quality, and there are no "bait and switch" methods of selling. No warranties or guarantees are necessary for anything one purchases or trades.

COMMERCE AND INDUSTRY

In commerce, there are no legal loopholes, no contracts or legal documents with evasive, misleading fine print or deliberately inaccurate estimates and workmanship, and no lawsuits.

In all financial and commercial transactions, a person's word (or handshake) is his or her bond. There is no need for complex legal contracts, and no attorneys are necessary to handle contracts, sales, distribution of estates, and the like.

Gold, silver, and precious metals and stones are in abundance as mediums of exchange and for use in jewelry, but there is no greedy grasping or hoarding of them.

I noticed when people travel for commerce or pleasure, there are no hotels or motels as we know them here. Rather, people stay in personally owned facilities much like our bed and breakfasts here, some being very large with many rooms and dining facilities. Guests do not pay for such lodgings because the owners offer lodging and meals as gifts of hospitality; they delight in humbly and selflessly serving their lodgers.

15

CHILDREN

> The wolf will romp with the lamb, the leopard sleep with the kid. Calf and lion will eat from the same trough, and a little child shall tend them.
>
> *—Isaiah 11:6, The Message*

> All your children will have God for their teacher— what a mentor for your children!
>
> *—Isaiah 54:13, The Message*

IN JESUS'S KINGDOM ON THE RESTORED EARTH, there are newborn babies, infants, children, and young people. They are not born there but arrive at those ages. Caring, nurturing, loving adults (not necessarily their mortal parents) care for them, feed them, clothe them, and instruct and teach them. They seem to grow to prime adulthood very quickly, all the while guided, directed, and cared for by various loving adults.

All children seem wise beyond their years but are still children, with running, jumping, playing with one another, screaming, yelling—their pleasant, playful sounds fill the air throughout heaven. As mentioned previously, Jesus is most often surrounded by children; He loves to play at their childhood games with them. He is great at hopscotch!

ABORTED AND ADOPTED

Throughout human history on old earth, multitudes of babies and infants were aborted. In God's kingdom on the restored earth, it is very poignant to see them reunited with their birth mothers; with full understanding of the events surrounding their abortions, I observed overwhelming joy and laughter as birth mothers and aborted babies were reunited.

The same is true with babies and children who were given up for adoption for various reasons. When reunited with their birth parent(s), there is great joy and many tears of happiness.

Although wise and knowledgeable, all children nevertheless exhibit joy, delight, wonder, and excitement, and a growing sense of adventure about the LIFE upon which they have now embarked. They do not attend school as such, but each has loving tutors and personal educators in all the sciences, arts, mathematics, earth's history, astronomy, the ways and works of God, and other learning disciplines.

Among children, there are no rowdy, lazy, rebellious, or negative attitudes about learning but a deep sense of gratitude and thankfulness for the infinite learning opportunities in heaven.

16

EDUCATION

This is what the prophets meant when they wrote, "And then they will all be personally taught by God."

—*John 6:45, The Message*

IN THE KINGDOM OF HEAVEN THERE ARE NUMEROUS God-centered places of learning in which one can pursue and study an infinite number of subjects and learning disciplines at all levels of understanding and all stages of awareness.

There are myriad opportunities to explore new, uncharted areas of study, ranging from the microuniverse, nanotechnology, astrophysics, and the entire macrouniverse. Also, people study in great depth the loving character, nature, and essence of the infinite Creator.

There doesn't seem to be any formal classroom education, which at its best here on old earth yields only the barest beginning or introduction of true and complete education. In Jesus's kingdom on the restored earth, people fill in their full education themselves (with the teaching enlightenment of God the Holy Spirit)—with the Bible being the foundational text of all knowledge and wisdom.

The sum of everything that every mortal human had ever learned or experienced on old earth was like a single grain of sand on all earth's beaches. In heaven, no one ever ceases learning, especially the great depths of the Bible's teachings.

Education is simply learning to discriminate between ideas of whatever one chooses to study, ranging from the microuniverse to the macrouniverse. All education is pleasurable and enjoyable, not dull, routine, or boring.

RESEARCH

Research in the hard sciences (such as engineering, chemistry, metallurgy, etc.) is fun, leading to an infinite number of developments in the character and nature of the universe and of God. Study in the social sciences (such as psychology, sociology, etc.) also leads to great progress in understanding the nature and character of both God and redeemed humanity. Such leads to deeper, more intimate relationships with God and with one another.

It seems God will ever be unveiling Himself to all redeemed and restored humanity, leading to even deeper love for Him. He already loves all humanity fully, but restored humanity is continually learning to respond to His love in return—constantly falling deeper and deeper in love with Him.

I observed technicians, researchers, and scientists using scanning microscopes capable of clearly revealing the working insides and components of individual atoms, disclosing a microuniverse comparatively as large or larger than the macrouniverse. It seems there are ever unfolding new microuniverses as well as the macrouniverse to explore. What is inside is larger than that which is outside.

There are vast research laboratories and centers to study—and unlock—the deep mysteries, secrets, and patterns of the universe, including seemingly infinite mathematical formulas, calculations, numbers, symbols, and equations—including fractals.

There is an interconnectedness and complexity of all fields of mathematics. Studies are based on the discovery of mathematics, not the invention of such.

Much research and study leads to harnessing many amazing new forms of energy previously unknown and untapped, all flowing from the all-powerful nature of God the Holy Spirit.

A few of the notable mathematicians and scientists Alaleel pointed out to me were Pythagorus, Aristotle, Euclid, Galileo, Newton, Maxwell, Einstein, Curie, Jonas Salk, Robert Oppenheimer, Hubble, Stephen Hawking, and others.

All work, all labor, all efforts, all studies, all learning, all teaching, and all research and development are to honor and laud Jesus for all He has done to redeem and restore all humankind to a right and proper relationship with God and for His great power by which all things in creation adhere, cohere, and consist.

17

THE UNIVERSE

> God! Let the cosmos praise your wonderful ways, the choir of holy angels sing anthems to your faithful ways! Search high and low, scan skies and land, you'll find nothing and no one quite like God.
>
> —*Psalm 89:5, The Message*

THERE ARE INNUMERABLE AND UNTOLD NATURAL and organic resources among all the meteorites and asteroids in our solar system alone—and even more, almost infinite resources beyond the boundaries of our relatively small system. Space exploration and mining are safely and routinely developed and operative in Jesus's kingdom of heaven.

SPACEPORTS AND SPACE STATIONS

I saw only a glimpse of this, but was astounded by all the activity, travel, and commerce among the many spaceports scattered throughout restored earth. They are not for airline travel, but for some other type of speedy stratospheric travel I did not comprehend.

I believe there are many large space stations, too, but saw only one of them, an immense one circling the earth. I somehow understood each station is for combined commerce, education, housing, tourism, recreation, and entertainment.

All of the hundreds of thousands of pieces of space debris that formerly circled old earth have been gathered and destroyed. The atmosphere of the restored earth (actually reaching to the stratosphere and beyond) is finally free and clear of such debris.

I was not permitted to observe many matters regarding space because if I reported about them, it would seem as if I was writing highly imaginative and speculative science fiction rather than simply reporting clearly the realities I observed.

UNIVERSAL TRAVEL

In addition, I felt I was seeing only the very small beginnings of some sort of eternal space program to carry God's Good News about Jesus to the far-flung reaches of the vast, unbounded universe. My memories of such matters are very dim, unclear, indistinct, and fuzzy to me—I think to keep me from speculating about such matters.

Generally, most beings travel throughout the universe at the speed of thought, whether traveling for pleasure, tourism, commerce, or on missions to tell others about all God has done in love for them through Jesus. I didn't observe more than the tiny "tip of the iceberg" about various other means of travel throughout the universe.

Perhaps as a visitor I was simply not permitted to observe or experience such universe-travel because it was far beyond my mortal powers of observation or comprehension; perhaps observing or experiencing it fully might have "blown my mind." I cannot even speculate about how such travel occurs; it just does.

There is no time travel to the past or to the future because there is no longer any time; all is absolutely simultaneous, making travel instantaneous between any locations in the universe. Again, I observed such phenomena, but I certainly don't understand how such phenomena occur in heaven. There, it seems very normal and routine; here, it is miraculous and magical.

God alone is able to travel between times; the kingdom's inhabitants are not able to do so. During my visit I had a feeling that heaven's inhabitants are not even fully aware that there exist past, present, and future times (as we understand them) since all is absolutely simultaneous to them. I'm not explaining that very well; it's simply beyond my comprehension.

THE MILKY WAY

The Milky Way is like a silver river running through eternal realms of space. On numerous occasions during my visit I saw Jesus (often with a dance troupe) dancing with abandonment and glee up and down the Milky Way—just out of sheer, unbridled joy of LIFE.

At times, He and the other dancers were huge beyond description while dancing, whirling, leaping, and pirouetting on that vast silver river. At the same time, both the dancers and the Milky Way were small enough that they seemed to be right in front of their audiences on restored earth.

God orchestrates the Aurora Borealis (Northern Lights) to stage massive, colorful displays, seen not only in the far northern hemisphere but throughout the world. They dance, weave, and sway to the sounds of celestial music.

In addition, colorful, gigantic, full rainbows are often seen, although there is no rainfall on restored earth. The rainbows pulsate and dance to the sounds of the same celestial music as does the Aurora Borealis.

SPACE PHENOMENA

Throughout the vast universe, black holes have been transformed into tunnels of light serving some purposes I could not begin to fathom. However, I did experience a faint inner awareness that such tunnels are passages between infinite dimensions and locales outside of and beyond time and space as we know and experience them here.

Each galaxy is home to various species of intelligent living beings, some redeemed by Jesus's universal sacrifice on old earth and some not needing redemption. God knows each species and loves them all with limitless love beyond measure. Each species is created in the image of God as humans are. To be created in the image of God means that one is a visible representation of the invisible God.

Dark matter in the universe has been replaced by some sort of light matter leading to a type of divine photosynthesis bringing more LIFE to all creation. The light matter is not overwhelmingly bright but is somewhat subdued and hazy. In a sense, universal darkness and semidarkness (including dark matter and dark energy) have been replaced by the light and LIFE of God.

18

VEGETATION AND TREES

So you'll go out in joy, you'll be led into a whole and complete life. The mountains and hills will lead the parade, bursting with song. All the trees of the forest will join the procession, exuberant with applause.

—*Isaiah 55:12, The Message*

VEGETATION

ALL FRUIT GROWING ON TREES AND BUSHES IS FREE, plentiful, and available simply for the picking to all inhabitants of heaven, both people and animals. The trees are not seasonal but are always green, leafy, and laden with abundant fruit, many of larger, luscious varieties never seen here on old earth.

Small, multicolored insects—especially both large and small gorgeous butterflies (some bigger than birds)—fly, buzz, crawl, dance, frolic, and play around the fruit, all the while singing sweet, soft, lilting songs of praise to their Creator.

Bees are always busy producing honey for human and animal consumption; they do not sting. Their buzzings are songs of praise to their Creator. There are no insects harmful to plants and no plant diseases. There are no thorns, thistles, brambles, nettles, or unwanted noxious weeds—and no poisonous vegetation.

All pesky flies, ticks, mosquitoes, gnats, spiders, bugs, termites, tree borers, molds, harmful plant bacteria, and other similar creatures formerly considered pests by humans on old earth are now cleaners who scour throughout the restored earth to rid it of tiny particulates, dirt, dust, and other types of natural debris.

In God's kingdom of heaven on the newly restored earth, it appears that all vegetation is self-sustaining and self-maintaining; for example, no one mows lawns—lawns maintain themselves. There are no rotten fruits and vegetables, and there is no blight, no dead trees, no plant diseases, no fallen leaves, nothing dead by drought or excessive heat or by destructive insects.

Hillsides, meadows, and forests display a thousand hues of green grass, ever enjoying that they are there to serve humans who tread upon them. When flattened or crushed, they grow back immediately.

All vegetation (plants, orchards, vineyards, flowers, trees, lawns, gardens, etc.) seems to be fully alive and fully aware, expressing some sort of unspoken joy that they can serve their Creator and feed and give pleasure to redeemed humankind and animals.

New, huge quantities of nutritious plant foods are now grown in restored earth's reconfigured seas and oceans, greatly multiplying food sources, usually planted, tended, and maintained by aquatic creatures. Aquatic plants ebb and flow in dances choreographed by currents and tides.

There are more than enough plant foods for all animals and humans, but somehow I never saw any wasted food or obesity. Somehow, God is able to balance supplies and demands for food throughout His kingdom on restored earth.

Plentiful harvests often come close to overtaking sowing and planting in rich, fertile soil, and from orchards and vineyards. In that fertile kingdom on earth, foods that are grown are of larger sizes and varieties than ever seen here.

There are vast public and private flower and vegetable gardens, kitchen gardens, and orchards. In many locales I saw acres and acres of crops stretching to the far horizons, all maintaining themselves. There are vast fields of grains and other crops waving in soft breezes.

Almost everywhere I looked, huge fields of flowers grow in maze-like patterns of seemingly wild profusion. The patterns constantly shift as the winds of the Spirit blow gently upon them. The slowly shifting patterns are the flowers' ways of praising and extolling God in flower languages.

Everywhere there is much greenery in innumerable shades and hues, dazzling beyond my description. Brightly colored flowers grow everywhere; they are beyond measure and comparison with any here on old earth, more beautiful than any ever beheld in our mortal lives here. There are more varieties of flowers than one can ever count.

The fields of flowers stretch into distances farther than my eyes could see. Children and animals play among them—the children picking bouquets and making flower chains. All flowers instantly grow back when plucked.

I never saw rain, only very light morning and evening dew and mist. All vegetation is watered by mists and underground springs, somehow fed by the River of LIFE no matter where the vegetation is located on the planet.

When I walked on lush grass, gazed at the beauty of a majestic spreading tree, smelled and appreciated the rich scents of flowers, and admired the sparkling, crystal clear waters, I could sense them communicating to me: "Thank you for letting us serve you and bring you pleasure; that is why our Creator made us."

All plant life, birds, insects, and other animals communicate with each other: trees to bushes, bushes to grass, grass to flowers, and so forth. Breezes and winds of the Spirit help them communicate, carrying messages from place to place—as well as seeds from place to place.

TREES

I noticed that some special unknown types of trees grow along the banks of all waters. For example, all along both shores of the River of LIFE, the trees produce luscious fruit at all times, the fruit being LIFE giving and healthful.

In lush forests, there are no deadfalls, no rotting vegetation, and no dead limbs. All forests are self-manicured and open to all for picnics, camping, strolling, and tourism visits. Many trees are massive, much larger and taller than the famed California Redwoods. There are many varieties of trees not known on old earth. For hiking and walking in forests, trees somehow seem to be able to shift and form shady aisles through which visitors can stroll and hike. Some trees are felled and used for cheery fires in fireplaces, for campfires, and for bonfires. Those trees seem to selflessly and willingly sacrifice themselves for human pleasure. There are no forest fires.

There are no dense, jungle-like forests with tangled undergrowth having harmful growth such as thorns and ensnaring vines.

I saw many people living in gorgeous, intricate, elaborate tree houses, with large tree branches serving as the paths between homes, villages, and neighborhoods high in the trees.

Arboreal animals live with and near humans among the trees, each species interacting and serving one another. Some of the larger arboreal animals delight in giving rides to young humans, swinging and leaping from branch to branch and tree to tree without any fear or danger.

As noted previously, there is no rainfall, but sometimes warm mists are seen; everything is somehow watered underground by rivers, creeks, and streams of LIFE along the banks of which grow trees of LIFE. Absolutely every growing piece of vegetation—down to individual blades of grass—receives the exact amount of moisture needed for maximum growth.

19

SPIRITUAL LIFE

Bread alone will not satisfy, but true life is found in every word, which constantly goes forth from God's mouth.

—Matthew 4:4, TPT

What you say, goes, God, and stays, as permanent as the heavens. Your truth never goes out of fashion; it's as up-to-date as the earth when the sun comes up. Your Word and truth are dependable as ever.

—Psalm 119:89–90, The Message

HERE ON OLD EARTH, AMONG ALMOST ALL religions much is said about how to develop and maintain one's spiritual life: reading holy books, meditating, memorizing, praying, attending religious services, maintaining spiritual disciplines, attending spiritual retreats and conferences, and the like.

In heaven, one's active spiritual life is simply a given; no one is spiritually lazy, causing their relationship with God to ebb and wane. Everyone is always spiritually alive without distractions and the downward pull of one's former sinful nature.

The Bible is constantly read, studied, and memorized according to each person's current state of awareness and present level of understanding. Each redeemed citizen holds his or her own understanding of the Bible, but never in a way that evokes arguments, bickering, and disagreements, only light-hearted and meaningful discussion. The Bible is the eternal, LIFE-giving reference guide for one's relationship with God and others.

THE BIBLE

There are no attempts to impose one's own views about the Bible or to control others. There is no such thing as religious denominationalism or only one true version or translation of the Bible. There is no religion at all—only deep, loving relationships with God and with one another, regardless of one's past relationships (or lack thereof) during their mortal lives.

The Bible is a deep, eternal Book, to be ever mined for its spiritual wealth and guidance as all people ever seek a deeper and deeper relationship with the God of the Bible— the infinite revelation of the infinite God.

Other great scriptures from other religions on old earth are read and studied, too, but primarily in the sense of how they relate to the Bible—how the Bible sheds light upon their teachings and clarifies them.

God's LIFE and energy are restored and replenished within people by consistent prayer, Bible reading and study, and by sharing spiritual and God-centric matters with others.

Such ongoing relationships with the Bible are not dull, boring chores or routines, but people are delighted to spend one-on-one communion with God through the awesome inner presence of the Holy Spirit sharing the meaning of the Bible with them.

As seen in our chapter heading, it is very real on restored earth that "People shall not live by food alone, but by every word proceeding from God" (Jesus's statement: Matthew 4:4). God's Eternal Word, the Bible, ever remains LIFE-giving and full of authority and power. Almost everywhere I looked, I often saw people reading and studying the Bible as individuals, in small groups, and in large meetings.

People on old earth have always seen "through a glass darkly" (1 Corinthians 13:12). In Jesus's kingdom on the restored earth, God the Holy Spirit (the author of the Bible) is able to fully explain deep, previously hidden, LIFE-giving truths of the Bible, never before able to be comprehended by readers and hearers in their limited mortal states.

INTIMATE SPIRITUAL RELATIONSHIPS

Every personal or group encounter always results in giving of oneself to others, blessing and being blessed, encouraging and uplifting one another. Spiritual interpersonal relationships in heaven are far deeper and more intimate than the most intimate relationships and camaraderie or spiritual fellowship ever experienced and felt here on old earth.

I saw relatively few church buildings or houses of worship—and they existed only for historical purposes and as museums. On the restored earth, one's relationships with God and others is 24/7, not requiring special times in special places set aside for worship. People, not buildings, are the eternal dwelling place of God.

As previously mentioned, however, there are many retreat centers scattered throughout restored earth where people go to develop deeper relationships with God and with others, and where they go to meditate, read, pray, and write privately.

None of heaven's inhabitants ever feel deep loneliness with all its devastating effects. That inner vacuum of loneliness in the human heart that mortals feel here, in heaven is filled to the full with the LIFE of God.

There is much reminiscing in heaven—remembering and visiting about good times, victories, exploits, breakthroughs, and all that Jesus has done for each person there. Not about "bad" experiences but only the good—the positive, joys, happy times, fun times.

It seemed almost as if all the bad had been forgotten, because redeemed people now fully understand that God has ultimately turned all bad—all that was evil—into good, as He has promised in the Bible to do. There is a pervasive sense that everything they had experienced in their mortal lives had been worth it all now that they were home.

As I noted earlier, no one is ever lonely, even though they may choose at times to be alone. Never again does anyone ever experience that deep, deep overwhelming loneliness often felt while mortal. Yes, there are episodes in heaven when people choose to be alone for various reasons (such as spiritual retreats or meditation), but they are never lonely.

All the legitimate longings, yearnings, and desires (including homesickness) that people experience on old earth are fulfilled in Jesus's kingdom on the restored earth. Heaven brings ultimate satisfaction.

All homesickness in both childhood and adulthood that people ever experienced here in their mortal lives is fulfilled in heaven, their true home. All God's redeemed and restored children know they are finally and truly home, never again to leave or mistakenly wander off to a "far country" (as the prodigal son did in Luke 15:11–32).

PUBLIC WORSHIP

Periodically, each inhabitant of heaven feels inwardly drawn to appear before God's throne to pay homage, to worship, to praise, and to swear devotion to Jesus who is the loving King of kings and Lord of lords. Thus, there are always great crowds of the King's loyal subjects gathered before His throne, but not all at once—except on rare occasions of planetwide or worldwide celebration.

20

NO SIN AND NO EVIL

We know that when Jesus was raised from the dead it was a signal of the end of death-as-the-end. Never again will death have the last word. When Jesus died, he took sin down with him, but alive he brings God down to us. From now on, think of it this way: sin speaks a dead language that means nothing to you; God speaks your mother tongue, and you hang on every word. You are dead to sin and alive to God. That's what Jesus did.

—*Romans 6:8–11, The Message*

He'll establish justice in the rabble of nations and settle disputes in faraway places. They'll trade in their swords for shovels, their spears for rakes and hoes. Nations will quit fighting each other, quit learning how to kill one another.

—*Micah 4:3, The Message*

RESULTS OF SIN ABOLISHED

ALL OLD EARTH'S WOES DIRECTLY RESULTING FROM
sin have simply ceased to exist on the newly restored earth—
and heaven's citizens actually have no memory of them. Sin
and all its horrible consequences have been eradicated. Sin
and evil have been totally overthrown, along with all their
ugly results!

Alaleel made it clear to me that in heaven there are
many situations, events, activities, and other actions that
don't exist there but that continue to exist here on old
earth due to the ongoing presence of sin generation after
generation.

Most of those ills that no longer exist in heaven
are conditions that continue to exist in this mortal life
because of sin, wrongdoing, and evil—all as results and
consequences of such.

All sin and *all* its results were eradicated and abolished
as God ushered in the kingdom of heaven on restored
earth. Perhaps you will find new hope in this life by looking
forward to being free of sin (and all its harmful, destructive
effects) in heaven.

At one time or another in this mortal life each of us
has been hurt by sin, either sin we've been engaged in or
sin others have foisted upon us. We've fallen prey to sin,
been saddened by it, bilked, deeply disappointed, betrayed,
wrongly accused, misunderstood, abandoned, ostracized,
wounded, overlooked, grieved, stolen from, diminished by
others, put down, cheated, hurt—by many earthly events,
situations, or people involving sin.

By reading about my visit, please take hope that when
you die and go to heaven, all events and situations resulting

from sin will be behind you and forgotten and never again will you be hurt by them; they are all replaced by great joy, wonderful comfort, and marvelous peace because of your new, sin-free LIFE in God's eternal kingdom realms.

HEALTH AND WHOLENESS

There are no physical, mental, or emotional sicknesses, diseases, illnesses, disabilities, accidents, or injuries in Jesus's kingdom. There are no genetic defects. There are no deformities, no missing limbs, and no one is crippled or malformed.

Because all the above sin-caused conditions are absent in heaven, there are no medical, mental health, rehabilitation, hospices, alcohol and drug treatment, or any similar facilities of any kind, civilian or military. There is finally no need for them—including medical and dental schools and medical, dental, and other health-care personnel.

I observed what it must finally be like to be healthy, whole, vital, and robust, although, as a visitor I did not experience such wholeness. For heaven's citizens, all past mortal illnesses are regarded as having been only light afflictions.

All citizens of Jesus's kingdom are now eternal beings and will never again undergo the heartbreaking wrenching and separations of physical dying and death.

NO CRIME OR LAW ENFORCEMENT

The Bible claims that basic human greed (the love of money, the lust for money) is the "root of all evil" (1 Timothy 6:10). Because greed no longer exists in Jesus's kingdom, there is no crime of any type there.

The ages-old condition of human slavery no longer exists on restored earth. All former slaves of any type and of any situations are now completely free! They hold no feelings of ill will, vengeance, or revenge against those who formerly enslaved them.

Also, there are no sexual crimes of any sort on restored earth! All former victims of such crimes are now healed and whole, living full, abundant, and rich lives in Jesus's kingdom. They have forgiven those who molested, abused, or preyed upon them.

There are no law enforcement agencies or prisons. There are no courts of law or judges and magistrates. There are no private investigators and no security guards at various commercial enterprises and institutions. There are no locks or other security devices to keep out interlopers, thieves, robbers, or burglars. There are no surveillance devices or cameras. And, of course, there is no watchful law enforcement presence anywhere.

There are no political assassinations, no drug wars, and no senseless killings. Serial killings are a thing of the past.

RENEWED HUMAN NATURE

There is no jealousy or envy. I did not perceive any signs of false pride or humility. No one—child or adult—ever exhibits tantrums or harmful negative theatrics, whining, or acting out.

I observed no age-related worries or fretting over problems such as baldness, age spots, wrinkles, weakness, arthritis, loss of control of various bodily functions, and the like, all associated with aging.

No one is ever jaded or cynical, sarcastic, or grouchy, or "down in the dumps." People do not scheme or plot to get even with someone else. There are no vendettas and no feuds. No one seeks vengeance against anyone.

Gossip, rumors, and lying do not exist. There is no bending or stretching the truth, no exaggeration, no withholding information to exert power over others. There is no prejudice or bias of any type.

No one ever again endures heartaches. There is no more sorrow or pain because of loved ones wandering astray or due to broken relationships.

I never observed anyone ever exhibiting anger, and never saw anyone fighting, arguing, squabbling, or holding grudges. There is no bullying, mocking, or name-calling.

There was much untold violence on old earth since the dawn of human history. There is absolutely no violence in heaven!

There are space agencies and operations, but all are for peaceful purposes and exploration. There are no spy satellites.

No one lives in fear of anyone else or of any government entity or agency. Only truth, openness, and honesty between all citizens prevail everywhere throughout the eternal realms.

In heaven, no one ever again feels threatened in any way by evil, wrongdoing, harm, or accident. There is no foreboding of something "bad" going to happen. Life is lived with complete trust and safety in God. No one need look behind him- or herself in dread, look over his or her shoulder in fear, or listen for the scary sounds of footsteps behind him or her in the dark.

There is no dread of the unknown or fear of an uncertain future or belief that something bad is bound to happen because it often seemed to be so in their past on old earth.

I was aware of pervasive, palpable peace transcending everything, with no distress, no worries, and no tension. Everyone and everything is finally free of the constant downward pull of human sin and all its results. Sin's incessant downward pull similar to the law of gravity has been abrogated and no longer exists. On the contrary, there is always the upward pull of God toward Himself through Jesus. Here in our mortal state of being, sin and sadness surround most of us most of the time and often prevails. In heaven, there is no sin or sadness; instead, there is perfect peace and joy.

NO WAR

All personal, local, regional, and international wars and conflicts have ceased. There are no weapons of warfare (nor weapons for hunting) except those found in historical museums; however, I did see some weapons used for target practice and competition.

There are no military-industrial complexes that research, design, and manufacture weapons. Nothing is designed or produced to inflict harm upon humans, animals, or plant life. Everything invented, created, or designed is for good, and for positive, encouraging, uplifting purposes.

Because there are no longer any wars, there is no need for any military schools, training or land, sea, or air personnel. However, I did observe ceremonial, uniformed guards and honor guards of various sorts but no actual, active military personnel.

How utterly amazing that the kingdom of God is without all the sin-based phenomena I've mentioned above. In one way or another, all of us here on old earth are bound by various types of sin fetters such as the above—fetters that will be removed from us in heaven, and we finally will be free from sin and all its hurtful consequences!

PERFECT JUSTICE AND GOVERNMENT

Perfect justice prevails throughout this fair heavenly realm, and I was given to understand that God's judgment and justice are mutually defined as: "He always makes all wrong things right."

In heaven, there are no politicians (including no elections or running for office) or rulers and the like, but certain people are appointed by God to serve under Him as elders worldwide to ensure that God's ordinances and decrees are carried out and fulfilled properly, not in the sense of enforcement, but to explain and teach them to newcomers.

There is a one-world government under God's sovereign rule, but some sort of national boundaries remain in place where citizens are voluntarily grouped primarily by salvation history and experience, not by race or ethnicity.

There is no competition among such nations, but merely fluid boundaries and divisions.

Flags of many former nations on old earth are still flown and respected in a manner that historically memorializes in positive ways the good deeds and heroism performed by and among the redeemed citizens of those former nations. Such flags are not merely symbolic to those honoring them, but they are deeply meaningful and representative of the people, not the governments, of those nations.

The cruel two-headed monster of religion and politics that plagued all people of all generations on old earth has been replaced by the Spirit of God fully alive in each of heaven's citizens and by God's sovereign, one-world government.

21

DYING AND DEATH

On signal from that trumpet from heaven, the dead will be up and out of their graves, beyond the reach of death, never to die again. At the same moment and in the same way, we'll all be changed. In the resurrection scheme of things, this has to happen: everything perishable taken off the shelves and replaced by the imperishable, this mortal replaced by the immortal. Then the saying will come true:

"Death swallowed by triumphant Life!
Who got the last word, oh, Death?
Oh, Death, who's afraid of you now?"

—*1 Corinthians 15:52–55, The Message*

THE BIBLE BOLDLY PROCLAIMS: "PRECIOUS IN GOD'S sight is the death of his saints!" (Psalm 116:15).

Leaving here—dying—is merely being born into a new place—the kingdom of heaven. Yes, there may be birth pangs and labor pains, but they're merely part of the birthing process into the eternal realms. The mortal baby being born here on old earth is unaware and does not fear its birth; when we die and leave here, we must not fear our birth into heaven, either.

On old earth there are God-mandated limits on each human life span. Human death occurs when God summons home the spirits of people. When that occurs, people's bodies and souls are then cremated or buried in the earth or at sea.

During my visit to heaven, I learned that death has nothing to do with the views held by most people in the medical and legal professions here on old earth that a person is considered to have died when the brain is dead. Rather, death occurs when one's spirit exits one's body, summoned home by God.

On one occasion, while talking with one of heaven's redeemed ones, he mentioned that, like him, many of heaven's citizens had finally arrived there at home by the skin of their teeth because they had chosen to run away from God while in their mortal state. "How did that happen?" I questioned.

He told me this story. "If you were on old earth and decided to go to New York City from Chicago, you would head east. But let's say about halfway to New York City, for some reason you decided to go the exact opposite direction—as far away as possible from New York City.

"So you turned around and headed due west. If you kept going, you would still end up in New York City because the earth is a sphere. Even a prodigal one such as I who had decided to run away from God to a 'far country' still ended up here in heaven. All roads—no matter their direction—lead home!"

Have you ever had the experience of having been away from home but returning after a lengthy absence because you became very homesick? When the closer you got to home the more excited and happy you became? One of heaven's redeemed citizens told me that's how it had been when because of her failing health on old earth, she began to realize her numbered days were about to cease, and she would soon be returning here to her true home.

She could still remember the excitement and joy of that brief time when she realized she would soon be making that transition from old earth to restored earth—finally returning home—in spite of pain involved in her birth into eternal realms.

I was told by another of heaven's citizens that to die means he simply returned to the wonderful place of his origin when he was created. Eons earlier, he left heaven at his appointed time to be born as a mortal human baby.

That was why so many mortal humans here longed for heaven, because it was their true home they left only for a brief time to make their appointed journey on old earth—to learn and experience all God wanted them to learn as mortals before returning home.

In heaven, I observed no infirmities of old age, no dying, and no death. Universal death was defeated on old earth once and for all when Jesus was triumphantly resurrected by the power of God the Holy Spirit and strode boldly back into eternal realms with all creation—including all humanity—in His victory procession!

I observed that, in some manner I could not understand, one's family and friends who had previously arrived in heaven, on occasions when necessary, gathered to assist in their loved one's final journey (much as a midwife might), welcoming the loved one home with great joy and much celebration.

OLD FRIENDS

I saw (but was not allowed to visit with) many people I had known and loved for a short while on old earth but whom I had lost track of (and even forgotten) down through the lengthening years. Of course, my visit to Jesus's kingdom made me eager to see them in person again and renew our lost acquaintances after I die and arrive in heaven.

Once on old earth I loved a dear childhood friend for seven years before my family moved out-of-state, and I lost track of him. I saw him during my visit! (Obviously he had died and was now in Jesus's kingdom.) Oh, how I would have liked to have greeted and hugged him. I'll finally be able to do that some bright morning when I arrive in heaven!

22

FINAL NOTES

> My visit, my observations, and my experiences in the kingdom of God on restored earth found that wondrous place to be a glorious kaleidoscope of sights, sounds, colors, people, objects, and activities—orderly disorder, nonrandom randomness, nonchaotic chaos with deep underlying purpose and meaning in all.
>
> —Bill Boylan

THE FOLLOWING NOTES ARE SIMPLY MY RECORDED, final observations that don't seem to fit nicely into any previous categories or chapters. If you find I reported some seeming contradictions or questionable observations, please forgive me; this report is as true and clear as I could make it, but much of what I observed and experienced was simply more than my human vocabulary could handle.

The heaven I visited was—I believe—in the future after

Jesus's return to fully establish His kingdom on earth—and after all humans had been resurrected from their sleep of death. My visit was to a future, fully restored earth.

It was not a pie in the sky unknown place somewhere beyond the blue in the sweet bye and bye. It was a literal, tangible, palpable eternal realm on the restored earth to which all humanity ultimately enters after their own resurrections from death.

EVERYTHING NOT RESTORED

As far as I could determine during my visit, not everything (in an absolute sense) is restored in Jesus's kingdom on the restored earth—only those things God sovereignly chose to restore or bring back to life.

For example, most banks are not restored in heaven—simply because there is no need for such facilities; however, some buildings formerly used as banks are now used for other purposes in Jesus's kingdom.

SEVEN WONDERS

One phenomenon I didn't mention elsewhere is that many such historical sites as, for example, the Seven Wonders of the ancient world are now tourist sites on restored earth, but they are not necessarily each in their former locations. Other great historical sites have been restored, for example: the Coliseum in Rome; the statues, monuments, and buildings of ancient Egypt; the great library of ancient Alexandria; the Great Wall of China, and other similar sites throughout the world. All notable archaeological ruins and artifacts are restored to their former states.

INVENTORS AND THEIR INVENTIONS

All notable inventions and their inventors are restored; the inventors are much-in-demand lecturers and authors who travel the world reenacting the scenarios surrounding their inventions within the eras in which they lived on old earth.

I believe I will only recall the totality of all I witnessed and experienced during my visit when I die and enter Jesus's kingdom of heaven on restored earth. I can envision myself exclaiming over and over, "Oh, yes, now I remember that from when I visited heaven!"

I feel it necessary to apologize if much of this material about my visit to heaven seems to be somewhat disconnected (and sometimes repetitive) fragments of memories of my visit.

But once I recorded all I was permitted to remember, I hope you find them somewhat a whole picture—like a completed jigsaw puzzle, yet never really complete because the eternal realms are unbounded, infinite, and limitless—as God is.

ALL WASTED YEARS RESTORED

As a highly personal note, while visiting those realms, I learned without shame—or rebuke by Jesus—that some of my years here on old earth had been wasted years due to sinful, wrong choices and decisions I made, but these are years that will be fully restored when it comes my time to die and return to heaven.

Envision the finest, happiest, most fulfilling day you've ever experienced in your mortal life. Now imagine that day's experience to be timeless in eternal realms. Picture the most beautiful scene you've ever observed on old earth. Now imagine that beauty—beyond imagining!—in heaven everywhere you look.

In heaven, all legitimate earthly hopes are totally realized and completely fulfilled—all those dreams, visions, and hopes you've experienced during long, lonely nights weeping on pillows wet with tears of disappointment and sorrow.

Here on old earth during my mortal lifetime, I've had brief, embryonic thoughts, quick glimpses, short mentions of heaven in the Bible, but now I understand Jesus's kingdom of heaven much more fully because of all my observations and experiences during my visit. The Bible references to heaven have become new to me!

Heaven is a land we've been solemnly promised by God's sworn oath He cannot deny. It's not a kingdom we merely long for based on our own merits we hope are good enough to get us there. It is God's promised place prepared for each of us based solely on Jesus's merits.

It is the true land of our nativity. In heaven, there is an eternal roll call to which each citizen shall answer: "Yes, here I am—present, whole, and accounted for … finally and permanently home where I belong!"

TRUE REST

At the time of their deaths, many people leave this mortal life extremely weary emotionally, physically tired, and worn out for various reasons; in Jesus's kingdom of heaven there is perfect contentment and sweet, longed-for rest—not idleness, laziness, or inactivity, but peace and freedom from stress while we engage in meaningful and purposeful activities. All our unfinished business as mortals is finally finished, resolved, and completed to God's satisfaction ... and ours.

Death, the tomb, and the grave are always distant memories behind those who are in heaven, never dreaded as being ahead of them as was the case during their mortal lives.

In the kingdom of heaven on restored earth there is no fretting about the past, no worries or misgivings about an unknown future, only LIFE in a joyful, peaceful *now*, Finally, one can fully focus on and live only in the now!

NO LOST SHEEP

No citizen of heaven is any longer a "lost sheep" who has strayed to a "distant country" (as did the prodigal son in Luke 15). Jesus, the Good and Great Shepherd, has sought out all His prodigal children, located and found them, placed them lovingly on His shoulders, and carried them back to heaven, their true pasture, nevermore to stray and become lost. As something to think about, no one on old earth ever "found" Jesus; He was never lost. Instead, Jesus finds us lost ones, redeems us, and brings us home. He searches for us and apprehends us by His relentless love.

PIECING THE MEMORIES TOGETHER

For a few days after my visit, I just went about my daily routines as if nothing unusual had occurred—except for a disturbing restlessness growing deep inside me.

Then, after a few blank days had passed, I remembered a small fragment of my experience in heaven. Then another ... and another ... and another. Slowly over the next three months everything came back to me in bits and pieces—segments—as pieces of a jigsaw puzzle—until the puzzle seemed complete.

On June 18, 2018—approximately three months after my visit to heaven—the memories stopped. When the memories ceased, most of my time for the next six weeks or so was spent pondering, clarifying, fleshing out, and writing the memories.

During those first three intense months after my visit, I carried a small notepad and pen with me so I could jot down notes as the memories returned—while they remained clear. During that time I amassed many, many pages of notes. Sometimes I did not even sleep, kept awake all night by jotting down returning memories.

Thereafter, as mentioned above, it took me approximately another six weeks to input them into my laptop computer and flesh them out into the whole report you are now reading or hearing about; that was approximately the latter part of July.

I don't know whether or not more memories will

continue to surface, but I have a sense that what you are reading or hearing is pretty much the sum of what God wanted me to remember and write down for me to relate to you.

With hindsight, I now feel this method of God's restoring my memories, my observations, and experiences in bits and pieces over a few months was His way of protecting my mind and emotions from overload.

If all the memories had returned to me in one huge swoosh as a flash flood, they might have overloaded my mortal mind and emotions. Even now after the passage of a few months since my visit, I am often overwhelmed when pondering some aspect of my visit, and sometimes I shed joyous tears during such moments. I find myself wanting to go home, but not in any suicidal sense; I'm just homesick for my true home that I was privileged to visit ahead of time!

NO FURTHER MEMORIES OF HEAVEN

As noted earlier, when I began editing and tweaking my final draft of this report in late July after my visit to Jesus's kingdom March 6, it seemed that I had remembered all God wanted me to remember.

On a few occasions since, I have tried to remember one thing or another about my visit to heaven, and to my surprise discovered that from the time of my visit until now (late July), I have not been able to remember by my own strivings anything about my visit. If God had not disclosed my memories to me and had me record them, it would be as though my visit had never occurred!

This report is merely scratching the surface of what heaven is like; it is only a small glimpse—only a slight peek. Only when each of us dies and makes our final journey to those eternal realms will we really come to know heaven and God.

I was keenly aware throughout my visit that heaven is a place that is continually renewed, restored, replenished, remade, and refurbished; nothing ever becomes old, worn out, or decayed.

Heaven's inhabitants are at home on the freshly restored earth, yet somehow free of it—not earthbound—instead, one with the larger cosmos, in tune with the harmonious and divinely interconnected entirety of the universe. I cannot begin to describe or explain the glorious freedom they experience in full relationship with the Creator and with all creation.

While on earth in human flesh, Jesus spoke of people having abundant LIFE. In heaven, it is finally so. All citizens of heaven have such LIFE, God's very own LIFE in eternal realms. All citizens of heaven possess that LIFE, more abundant than ever experienced or imagined in their mortal state.

Because I am still a mortal locked into and restricted by the limitations of time and space, it was extremely difficult for me to adjust to visiting a place where there was no time and space as we experience it here.

LENGTH OF MY VISIT

Those few family members and friends who presently know about my visit have asked me how long I feel my visit to heaven lasted. I honestly don't know. My wristwatch indicated I returned about a half hour after I left.

However, during my visit it seemed as though I was there many months—or even longer. Since there is no passage of time in heaven, I suppose it's a moot point; I may have been gone only a half hour in chronological time, but I may have been in heaven a thousand years. Neither of those lengths of time holds any meaning because everything is absolutely simultaneous in heaven. Jesus's kingdom on the restored earth has no spatial distances or passages of time as we understand them.

I visited eternal realms, places wholly different from here—yet it was still earth. Heaven is altogether a wholly other dimension very difficult to fully experience, to observe, and to describe with my limited human language.

ALL THINGS ALWAYS NEW

The very air and atmosphere in heaven seems always to be alive with excitement, expectation, and anticipation. Everything is always new, to be fully embraced without fear of an unknown future. Often, there is almost a breathless hush of anticipation in the air, not of something to occur in the future, but of exciting situations and events happening in the eternal NOW.

On old earth people often have deep, vague, homesick feelings for a place they cannot remember, having been created there before memory, in eternity, before coming here in this mortal life to the tiniest segment of time out of eternity.

EVERYTHING INTERCONNECTED

This is very difficult to explain. All redeemed humans in heaven have lengthy biological chains spanning eons of human history, as well as spiritual chains reaching back to Jesus—and farther, clear back to creation.

Also, all have a divine interconnectedness ever growing and expanding as they share God's love through Jesus with others who, in turn, share with others, and so on, spanning centuries and generations both past and future. In heaven, all those chains and connections are clearly known and experienced in great celebratory reunions!

When I attempt to explain that, what comes to mind is the marking on a great-uncle's tombstone in our family cemetery not very far from where I live, which might help you understand what I'm attempting to write: "Another link is broken in our family band, but a golden chain is forming in a better land."

THOSE WHO HAVE ALREADY DIED

For years I have maintained in my personal journal a list of my friends, acquaintances, and family members who have died. Presently, there are over two hundred names on that listing! During my visit to heaven, I saw all those people who were in my listing—although I was not allowed to interact with them until I die and enter that kingdom on the restored earth.

I observed that all of those on my listing seemed somehow to be faintly aware of my presence while I was near them during my visit, as though I were standing somewhere in the shadows nearby. I somehow knew they were remembering me when my visit brought me near them; they thought of me and prayed for me and spoke of eagerly awaiting my coming there to join them.

MY SISTER AND DAUGHTER

As Alaleel launched us on my visit I secretly wished I would get to see my sister and best friend, Bobbie, and my newborn daughter, Heather, who lived only a few moments after she was born.

I did see them! But only for a few, all-too-brief seconds. I wanted so much to greet them, hug them, and tell them I love them and how very much I missed them through the lengthening years of my earthly pilgrimage, but I was not permitted to do so. I was really saddened—even a little angry!—that I saw them so briefly. But at least I did get to see them.

They both appeared to be in their midthirties in mortal years of age. They were stately, luminescent, glowing, regal, and oh, so beautiful! I don't think they were aware of my visit, but I did have a strange sensation they were actively waiting for me to join them upon my homecoming. I am at peace, having briefly sensed their anticipation.

NEW NAMES ON WHITE STONES

In the Bible, there's a reference (Revelation 2:17) about a white stone with a new name written on it. In my mind and spirit, I have long struggled with that reference, wondering whether it was past, present, future, literal, figurative, metaphorical—

But during my visit to Jesus's heavenly kingdom, I noticed His use of white stones. When people die and enter heaven, Jesus is always the first to greet them personally, welcoming them, hugging them, and visiting with them at length.

In each instance when He welcomes a newcomer to His kingdom, He removes a small white stone from one of His pockets, engraves something on it (I presume it is a new name) with His finger, and hands it to the newcomer.

Upon glancing at the new name engraved on the stone, the person receiving it usually weeps with joy when he or she seems to grasp the full meaning of his or her new name; I sensed that the new name carries deep, deep meaning about the new, transformed character and nature of the person to whom Jesus hands the stone.

Later during my visit I often observed people taking the stones out of their pockets and discussing with others at length their new names; each person seems to know his or her new name is distinct and unique, perfectly describing who he or she is and what his or her role is in the new LIFE. These events seemed to pretty well answer my long-standing questions about that reference in the Bible about a white stone with a new name inscribed on it.

WELCOME HOME!

Upon our mortal deaths (however, whenever, and wherever that will occur for each of us), the first Person we will encounter after our resurrections will be Jesus; I know He will warmly greet each of us—and hug us!—welcoming us to His newly renewed and restored kingdom of God on earth.

Next, we will be welcomed home by family and friends whom we have loved—and missed—here since their deaths. For me (as I mentioned previously), I especially long to be greeted and hugged by my sister, Bobbie, and by my newborn daughter, Heather.

PLACES I LONG TO VISIT

Afterward, I long to visit two locations on the restored earth, two locations that have been deeply meaningful and significant during my mortal life here on old earth. I'm assuming those locations will still exist on restored earth, although I didn't see them during my visit to heaven.

The first location is a relatively small peak named Boylan's Peak near the little bedroom community of Piedmont, South Dakota, on the eastern edge of the famed Black Hills, a well-known tourism area.

Boylan's Peak has long been part of the Boylan family property. As a child and youth (and sometimes even as an adult), I spent countless happy hours hiking up and down—and playing on and around—Boylan's Peak.

Many times I simply sat near the summit of the peak and watched the ranching endeavors in the fields below, people traveling on the roads, and activities in the small community of Piedmont a half mile or so to the west.

Boylan's Peak has always been a safe place for me, where I could escape some of the negative events and unpredictable changes in my life—and a place to read, pray, meditate, and reflect in general about my life.

Just as a point of amusement, not long before she died, my mother disclosed to me that I was conceived on the dirt floor of a building near Boylan's Peak! That building is still there, but they haven't yet erected a statue of me in front of it to commemorate my conception.

The second location I want to visit is Spokane, Washington. It was there I was spiritually conceived and born into Jesus's coming kingdom while I was stationed there as a young man in the military service of the United States. After being "born from above" (as Jesus termed it), Spokane was also the place of my spiritual infancy for the first few months of my new LIFE.

If a renewed and restored Spokane exists on the restored earth, I would love to visit there accompanied by Jesus and have Him disclose to me all the events of my previous life that He orchestrated behind the scenes leading up to my second birth and then all that occurred in my life there those few months subsequent to my second birth. I want to hear my entire mortal life's story in Jesus's own words as He perceived and orchestrated it.

After being greeted by Jesus and by my family and friends; after visiting Boylan's Peak and Spokane, then I want to wander and roam the universe—God's great playground, as someone has put it.

I deeply appreciate and love the mortal life God has allowed me to live here on old earth, even with all its unpleasant experiences; it has been a very ordinary—yet amazing!—life loving and serving the EXTRAordinary God!

HEAVENLY MINDED—EARTHLY GOOD

It is sometimes said that there are people who are so heavenly minded that they are no earthly good; that type of person is a rarity. The truth of the matter is that generally speaking throughout human history those people who truly have been heavenly minded are the ones who have done the best and the most good for others here on old earth.

Both history and much research has shown that most good works have been initiated and performed by those in all nations and all eras who have a solid hope in a good LIFE to come!

Those who live for this life only are often paralyzed and stymied by feeling life is random, chaotic, meaningless, has no purpose, and promises no hope for the future.

Having visited heaven, I now have much more peace, contentment, and hope in LIFE to come in eternal realms (Titus 1:2 and Hebrews 6:19) as I look forward to becoming an immortal citizen of the kingdom of God on the renewed, replenished, and fully restored earth.

THE ETERNAL CROSS EVENT

Just before my visit to heaven concluded and I returned, my guide, Alaleel, solemnly told me to remember that the cross upon which Jesus died stands solidly anchored in both time and eternal realms, towering over all creation.

One does not see the cross, per se, in heaven, but it is always there, always present, yet always in the background, always reminding all citizens of heaven that it is through and by means of the all-redeeming, substitutionary work of the One who died on that cross they have come to be heaven's citizens.

The cross is not so much a symbol of death, excruciating pain, agony, and unspeakable torture as it is God's instrument and means of victory and triumph inseparably connected eternally with Jesus's resurrection and return to heaven.

Yes, everything in all creation is joined together by the cross upon which Jesus suffered, bled, and died. The cross event is the capstone of all creation.

And, yes, Jesus is the sole means by which people enter heaven upon their deaths—even though they may have never even heard of Him before they died; their destination, though often unknown by them, has always been heaven.

God's love is boundless, beyond measure, and eternal; the cross event resulting from that love is universal. This was the final memory that returned to me a few months after I returned from my visit to heaven—the final piece of the jigsaw puzzle—after which I was finally able to complete this report of my visit to heaven that occurred on March 6, 2018.

HOPE, MEANING, AND FULFILLED PURPOSE

Finally ... please remember that in my opening notes in chapter 1, I wrote about hope, meaning, and purpose in life.

A few years ago a book titled *The Purpose Driven Life* became an international best seller; it helped millions of people find new purpose and meaning in their lives; people just don't do well in this life without meaning, purpose, and hope.

If you've struggled to find meaning and purpose for your life, please know that in Jesus's kingdom on the restored earth, there is no longer the random chaos in this life that causes many people to feel they have no purpose and that there is no meaning to their lives.

Instead, on restored earth, everything you do, think, and say will have purpose and meaning; you'll have eternal purpose and meaning to your LIFE linked with God's purposes for you in eternal realms.

And all your legitimate desires and hopes in this life are finally fulfilled in heaven! There you will finally find the ultimate meaning and purpose that you have sought for so long!

The details of God's ultimate meaning and purpose for your life will be custom tailored by God just for you. But for each of us, a large part of that meaning and purpose will be to carry God's Good News about His universal restoration through Jesus to the far-flung reaches of the universe ... and beyond.

We will ever be ambassadors of universal redemption and restoration to the entire universe—limitless, measureless, boundless, and without end!

Since my visit, Jesus's kingdom on restored earth is now more real to me than my existence here on old earth! I'm quite content to remain here "until my days shall know their number" (from an old gospel song) when I die, but this is no longer my true home!

EPILOGUE

HAVING READ THIS REPORT ABOUT MY VISIT TO Jesus's kingdom on restored earth, you might be thinking or asking, "That's interesting and all well and good, but what about God's restoration of things I need in my life now, while I'm still alive here on old earth? I have needs in my relationships, financial needs, needs for physical, mental, and emotional healing—all sorts of needs now, not in some far-off kingdom of God. Can—will—God fulfill the needs I have in this life?"

All I can write to answer such questions is what God says in His eternal word, the Bible: "I am convinced that God will fully satisfy every need you have [in this life], for I have seen the abundant riches of glory revealed to me through the anointed One, Jesus Christ!" (Philippians 4:19, TPT; brackets mine).

God's satisfying our needs does come with some conditions, however. We must have a personal relationship with Him through Jesus—not religion, but a relationship. We must understand the differences between our needs and wants (sometimes—not always—they are one and the same, but most often they are not); God does not promise to fulfill our wants, only our needs. Usually, God satisfies our needs primarily so we can share what He provides us with others having similar needs—not to hoard or amass "stuff" for ourselves. Finally, sometimes God's supply for our needs whizzes right on by us because we're not really expecting Him to fulfill our needs.

ABOUT THE AUTHOR

SOME WHO READ THIS BOOK MIGHT ASK, "WHO IS Bill Boylan?" Please understand very clearly that I'm just an ordinary man, a very nondescript, normal person. My wife and I have had a loving marriage for almost forty years. I have three biological children and one stepdaughter, three grandchildren, and five great-grandchildren.

There is nothing special or outstanding about me. I don't stand out in a crowd. I'm very "generic." I'm not tall and handsome; I'm not very smart, and I'm not very wise at times.

I live in a modest home on a quiet residential street in the relatively small community of Rapid City, South Dakota, near the beautiful Black Hills. The world-famous Mount Rushmore is about twenty-five miles from our home.

I pay my household expenses every month, help clean our house, wash most of our dishes, assist with our laundry, make the bed many mornings, drive a twenty-year-old pickup, and wear jeans and a sweatshirt or T-shirt most of the time. I get sick and grouchy from time to time. I love to watch silly sitcoms on television.

My hobbies are reading and occasionally hiking in the nearby Black Hills; I'm a regular mall-walker, but sometimes also walk on a nearby outdoor walking path with my wife and dogs, Piper and Zack.

My roots go down deep in this locale. My brother and his wife live nearby on the cattle ranch originally homesteaded by my great-grandparents in the 1870s.

Most of my working years were spent as a public school teacher, as a medical administrator, and as a tough staff sergeant in the US Air Force, the active Air Force Reserve, and the Air National Guard; and as a sergeant first class in the full-time Army National Guard.

I'm so very ordinary that it was an extremely difficult task for me to find appropriate words to describe to you my visit to heaven—to describe the indescribable.

I can be contacted through this publisher or by e-mail at leservices38@yahoo.com.